MAKING YOUR HOME
meaningful

BRE DOUCETTE

TEN PEAKS PRESS®
EUGENE, OR

Cover design by Nicole Dougherty
Interior design by Faceout Studio, Paul Nielsen
Photography by Bre Doucette
Interior line art © MOJX Studio / Shutterstock

For bulk or special sales, please call 1-800-547-8979. Email: CustomerService@hhpbooks.com

 TEN PEAKS PRESS is a federally registered trademark of The Hawkins Children's LLC.
Harvest House Publishers, Inc., is the exclusive licensee of this trademark.

Making Your Home Meaningful

Copyright © 2025 by Bre Doucette
Published by Ten Peaks Press, an imprint of Harvest House Publishers
Eugene, Oregon 97408

ISBN 978-0-7369-8972-5 (pbk.)
ISBN 978-0-7369-8973-2 (eBook)

Library of Congress Control Number: 2024945841

Printed in China

25 26 27 28 29 30 31 32 33 / LP–FO / 10 9 8 7 6 5 4 3 2 1

To the *Rooms for Rent* blog community, for sharing in the excitement and joy that go into creating a meaningful home and for allowing me the chance to encourage you to love the space you live in. From the bottom of my heart: Thank you!

nouse Style

CONTENTS

—

MAKING YOUR HOME MEANINGFUL

What is it about a certain type of home that captures your attention and awakens your curiosity? You know, the kind of home you see when flipping through a magazine or scrolling Instagram or Pinterest that stops you in your tracks. The home that, if you were to peek inside the front door, would have you longing to look into every room, and where every corner you ventured into held your full attention and invited you to see more.

The homes where we feel we truly belong are those that welcome us in and seem to tell us a story through the photos and artwork hanging on the walls and the decorative pieces that have been thoughtfully put on display. They draw us in as if to whisper, "Come and stay awhile," beckoning us to celebrate life and the season we're in.

Such a warm invitation is hard to resist!

Creating a meaningful home isn't about attaining a picture-perfect living room or a Pinterest-worthy kitchen. It's about creating a space that is meaningful to you and anyone you share it with. We each have our own individual story to tell—who we are, where we're from, what personally inspires us and makes us unique. We all long for a place where we can share our cherished traditions and memories...the treasures of the heart we hope to pass down to future generations or share with our friends. With an overall vision and some pieces perfect for your personal style, you can create your own ideal environment, one room at a time and one season at a time.

In part 1 of this book, you'll discover how to actually create your dream home that will take you effortlessly from season to season.

You'll figure out your own personal style, learn how to choose meaningful accessories, and determine the best place to start making your home a reflection of who you are and what you care about. You'll also be introduced to some foundational decorating techniques/formulas/staples so you can feel a little more confident as you go about creating a meaningful home. In part 2, you'll discover ways to bring the beauty of the seasons and their inspiration into your rooms—both indoors and out. Sometimes seasonal decorating can be consumed by the holidays, so we'll address the art of adding simple but meaningful seasonal touches. You'll also be introduced to my seasonal decorating favorites, along with simple DIYs that will leave you feeling inspired—and not overwhelmed—all season long.

My hope is that you will use this book as an inspirational field guide to help you cultivate your own true style and reflect it throughout your home as you celebrate the beauty of each season. I can't wait to go on this journey with you!

Creating a meaningful home is about creating a space that is meaningful to you and anyone you share it with.

Part 1

Creating Your Dream Home

Any home can be transformed into a place that is meaningful. It's true! You may not be living in your dream home right now, or perhaps your home was once your dream but it's lost that spark over the years. Whether you're renting a one-bedroom apartment or own your own house and property, I'm here to tell you that your home *can* be turned into a place that feels like you, serves your current life, and offers the beauty, inspiration, and comfort you desire.

If you feel like you're unsure of your decorating style or have no clue how to begin curating your own unique look, I'm here to help get you started. Knowing where to begin can feel a bit daunting in the beginning when so many questions emerge: *How do I choose the best colors? What is my design style? Is there a focal point in each space? Wait—what's a focal point?* But I promise you, it doesn't have to be intimidating. You can do this! Together, let's kick off the journey to creating a dream home you truly love.

PERSONAL STYLE

Your goal is to create a space that not only makes you feel comfortable but also truly reflects who you are and what you love.

DETERMINE WHERE TO START

Every time I get ready to decorate a space, whether it's a new home or a place I've lived in for years, I begin by identifying what the space needs. I am a list maker, so I get out a pen and paper and write down the needs for each room or area, including everything I want to change or improve. Is the room in need of a new paint color? A particular category or style of furniture? What improvements do I wish to make, such as a new light fixture, or perhaps a wall treatment to add in some character? This helps me zero in on where to start and sets a priority order for getting things done.

Regardless of the size and scope of the improvements you want to make, writing them down in list form helps you determine where to start and provides you with a bird's-eye view of your goals for the space.

If you're totally confused about where to begin, just pick a room. It's much easier to make decisions for one room versus tackling an entire house. Ask yourself, *Which room am I the most dissatisfied with at the moment?* And then start there.

Now that you've picked a room to work on, ask yourself how this room currently feels to you. Do you enjoy spending time in it? Is there anything that's currently working well in the space? What bothers you the most about this room—the furniture arrangement, the colors, the decor? Is there a certain look or style you want to come through in the design? Writing down any notes will help, even if you aren't exactly sure yet of the "style" you want. (Don't worry—we'll talk more about that in an upcoming section.)

Now, I ask this next question only because I know how much of an impact the answer can make: When is the last time you gave this space a deep clean? Before you start making big changes and adding in beautiful decor, you need to purge the unnecessary items that no longer serve you, the space, or your chosen style. As you're deep cleaning the room, decide what stays, what goes, and what would work better in another area. The gift of a clean slate will go far toward transforming your house into your dream home.

Sample Project List

To give you some inspiration and get you started, here is one of my to-do lists from a recent round of redecorating a bedroom:

Paint the walls—I used White Heron by Benjamin Moore.

Hang curtain rods and curtains.

Add two throw pillows to the bed.

Paint the dresser.

Hang pictures on the walls.

Purchase matching bedside table lamps.

Order a faux tree for the corner seating area.

Replace the area rug with one that has a subtle floral pattern.

Which room will you choose to begin with?
What excites you most about getting started
with your home transformation?

FIGURE OUT YOUR PERSONAL STYLE

It may sound obvious, but your personal style should look and feel like *you*. While you may appreciate how others decorate their homes and marvel at how all their elements have come together, remember that your style will have its own essence. And your goal is to create a space that not only makes you feel comfortable but also truly reflects who you are and what you love.

It's easy to be influenced by design trends, but the more you know about your own personal design style, the easier it will be to determine which trends you'll want to incorporate into your home and which trends are better left to admire in someone else's home. The truth is, you're probably tapping into your own design style more than you think!

CHECK YOUR CLOSET.

The clothes you buy and the outfits you put together daily can reveal a lot about your personal style. Take note of your favorite clothing items and combinations. Pretend you're describing them to me, and don't leave out any details. Are there certain colors you're drawn to? How would you describe your favorite look? Is it dressy or casual? What patterns and trends do you embrace?

Now, look around your home. Do you see any of the same colors, patterns, and styles showing up there? If not, write down what appears most in your wardrobe, because these are things that you will want to consider incorporating into your decor.

DRAW INSPIRATION FROM YOUR FAVORITE PLACES.

Do you have a love for the beach? Do the mountains call to you? Where is your family from? Your personal style can showcase the places that have meaning—and memories—for you. As a child growing up in New England, I frequented the beach in the summers; now, I decorate my home with the shells and stones I've collected at the shore with my kids. These treasures bring both beauty and nostalgia to our home.

Do you have a place you love to visit? Do you have mementos or souvenirs you brought back with you? Put them out on display. Also consider including places you're inspired by and one day hope to visit. Maybe a tour of Italy is on your wish list and the colors of Tuscany become a part of your backdrop. We will talk more about this later, but remember that decorating with items from your favorite places is a great way to reflect your personal style.

REFLECT YOUR STORY.

Your personal style comes through when you express your story and yourself in your surroundings. What do you have in your home that reflects the things you love, your hobbies and interests—both ones you had as a child or have now as an adult—your family's stories and passions? As you take a new look at your spaces, imagine how you might add decor that reflects your story.

There are no home decor police who will come knocking on your door to tell you that you've done it all wrong. So, let's shake off any fears that you're going to mess things up and give yourself permission to try unconventional things, follow your preferences rather than trends, and look to your own life for inspiration.

Have you thought about your story in
relation to your personal style?

CREATE MOOD & FIND INSPIRATION

Now that you've begun to identify your personal decorating style, it's time to focus on how you want your space to look and feel—as well as how it *makes you* feel. I'd been using the word "farmhouse" for years to describe my personal decorating style. Long before there were fixer-upper shows or store shelves filled with this style of accessories, I was stuck trying to describe what I liked, which was not really modern, yet not fully traditional—a cottage-like/eclectic style. The truth is, my tastes never really fit into a precise style category. They still don't! But I'm here to tell you that you don't have to fit your personal preferences under the current labels of different design styles before you can start making your home meaningful.

Whether or not your favorite look falls perfectly into a design category, figuring out how you want your space to feel may be the most helpful factor when choosing colors and accessories. First, think about the overall mood you want the space to reflect. Are you going for a light and casual vibe, or are you leaning more toward a moody and cozy environment? Do you prefer a playful space with unconventional pieces, or do you long for a formal area with muted tones that invoke quiet and solitude? Don't overthink it. Instead, do this simple exercise, either right here or in a notebook or file you are using for your home projects.

What three words describe the mood you want to create in your home?

You might realize that you want a different mood for each room of your house. Why not? That's totally fine! Once you've figured out your signature design style, you will be able to achieve the same cohesiveness throughout your entire home, even if the actual manifestation of that style varies according to the mood of each room.

Thanks to the seemingly endless source of social media offerings at our fingertips, we have access to thousands of photos for home-decorating inspiration. Gone are the days of cutting out pictures from magazines and pinning them to a board (although I actually still prefer this method). Social media allows us to browse beautiful rooms to our heart's content, all with the swipe of our finger. Take time doing this. Have fun. Explore design and decor looks and moods you haven't considered before. Mentally deconstruct images to evaluate why you like or dislike them.

Once you've chosen which room in your home to start with, compile a handful of inspiration photos that are your absolute favorites. You don't have to love every single detail in the images, but ideally you've collected an assortment of photos that showcase what you love most.

This process helped me pull the trigger in deciding to paint my walls white six years ago. I know it might sound silly coming from the girl who loves to paint, but you might be surprised to learn how intimidated I was to paint my walls white. White isn't really known for creating the warm and inviting space I am typically after. However, after compiling a collection of inspiration photos for my own living room, there was one thing they all had in common: white walls. I was surprised—and then convinced. I took the leap, and I've been painting my walls white ever since.

Write down the similarities that show up again and again in your inspiration images. Also write down anything else you notice about these spaces. Do certain materials or finishes repeatedly appear? Perhaps it's a similar paint color being used on the walls? Or the same style rug? What accent colors do you see on repeat in your inspiration rooms? What draws your eye—in a good way—when you first glance at each image? Create those lists, and then spend time reviewing them. Remember, you want to focus in on a few key elements that make your space meaningful to *you*.

Are you ready to change the mood of your home?
Are you surprised by which elements you're most drawn
to as you gather dream-home inspiration from images?

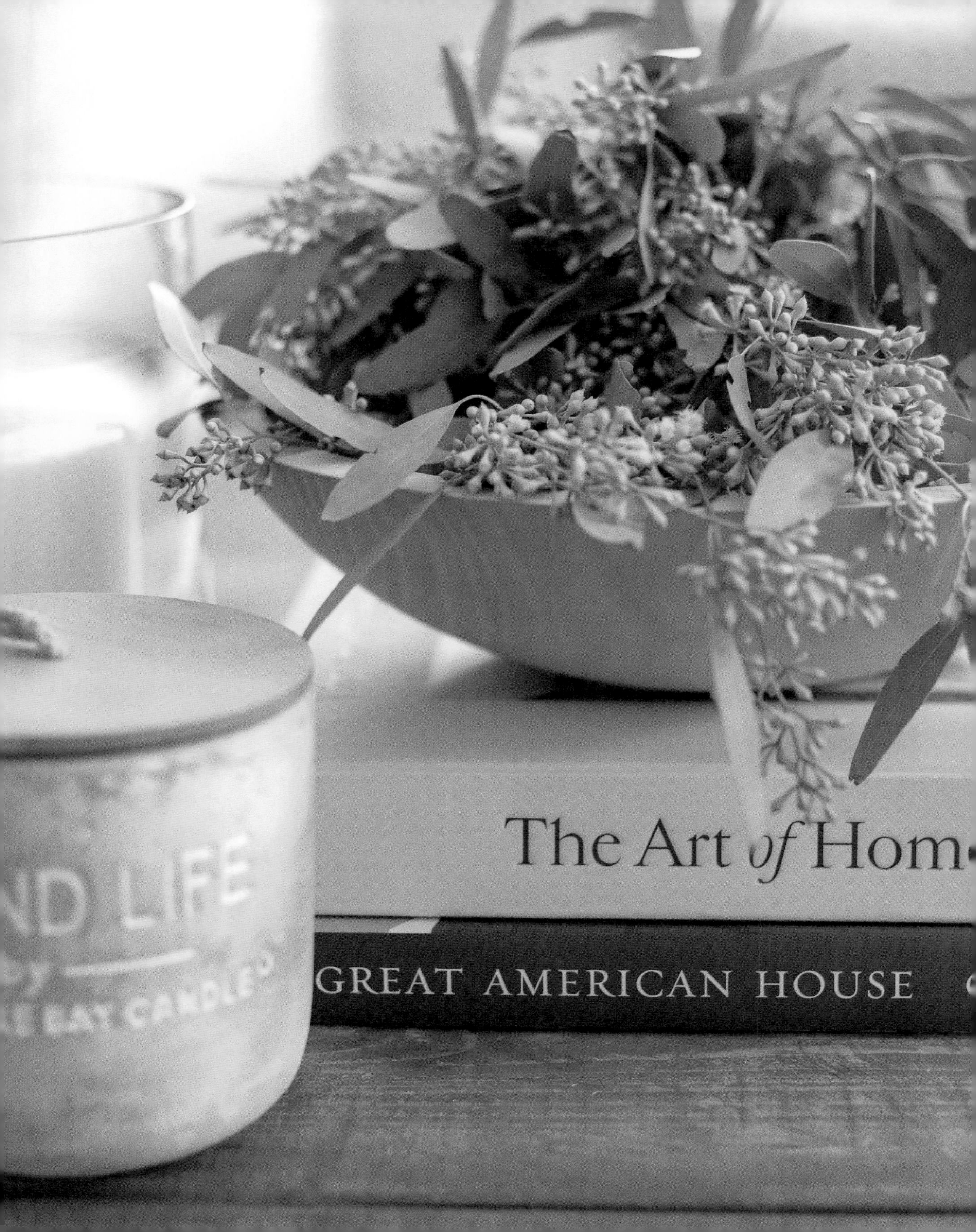
The Art of
GREAT AMERICAN HOUSE

PLAN YOUR
COLOR PALETTE

Let's talk color! Color shows up in our homes through the artwork, accessories, textiles, and paints we choose. From high-contrast bold tones to softer muted hues, color impacts how your home looks and feels. Earlier, you identified the mood you want for your space. Now, you can use color to help evoke that mood. Remember those inspirational photos I suggested you compile? Take a look at them again. Are any of the rooms you love painted the same color or tone? Make a note of it! Trust that what draws your eye and heart is what you want.

I love to look through paint chips and compare shades and undertones, but I realize not everyone enjoys this process. It can be daunting—there are *so* many choices! Here's my best advice for making the process a simpler *and* more fun and fruitful pursuit.

◆ Narrow down your list of possible colors to three to five options. If you choose too many, you'll end up frozen by indecision—or worse, you'll select a questionable color that doesn't complement your home or your style.

◆ Once you've narrowed it down to a few colors, research the paints online. Googling a specific paint color by name and brand will show photo results that will help you assess the color in different lighting and settings. Scroll through the photos and determine if the paint's different appearances still suit your goals.

◆ Decide on your top three and purchase those paint samples. This way you can test out the paint brand and the color in your home. I like to apply paint samples to a few different spots around a room so I can see how it looks in natural light at various times of the day. We don't typically think about the direction our home is facing, but when you start testing out paints, you realize how much of an impact the baseline light has on how the color looks in a room. I have tried multiple paint samples in the homes we've lived in, and even some of the top designer choices have come across as reading too pink or yellow in my home.

◆ Consider your favorite color as you make decisions. (Think back to the assessment of your favorite wardrobe pieces and the color represented there.) Then determine how to incorporate that color either centrally on your walls or as an accent color.

While my favorite color to decorate with is white, I don't want everything in the room to be white. My clothing choices show I have a fondness for blue, so that is the accent color I use for decorating accessories, smaller pieces of furniture, throw pillows, and other textiles.

By bringing your favorite color into your rooms through smaller items, you can easily introduce a new color scheme when you want to change things up.

I like to look to nature and the season we're in to determine how bold or subtle I want my colors to be. I'm also not afraid to edit my space. When I finally embraced white walls, I realized my love for white decor resulted in a space that was void of color. I started to incorporate some softer shades of blue and muted green (my third favorite color) until I felt the right balance. These colors are found on repeat in my home, creating a cohesive look from room to room.

Are the colors you are drawn to warm or cool in tone?
Go to a paint store and select a swatch that features a
color you like. Look at the other tones on the swatch
and determine how soft or bold you prefer the color to be.
Don't worry about which colors are trending.
Stay true to what you love because if you like it, it
will probably feel timeless in your home.

A LOVELY LIFE   MICHAELS

COZY MINIMALIST HOME   *Myquillyn Smith*

HISTORY REINTERPRETED   PATRICK AHEARN

Lived-In Style   KJ NASSAUER

Nora Murphy's Country House Style

THE GIFT O

MORE I

VISIONS O

EDIT (AND SHOP!) WHAT YOU HAVE

Now that you've identified the mood and color palette you want, it's time to take a closer look at what you have in your space currently. Does your current decor and furniture style support the look you're after? Even if you love how you decorated the space years ago, it may not reflect your personal design style now. But don't panic—maybe all you need are a few simple tweaks to breathe new life into your home. Or perhaps as you evaluate the current state of your rooms, you realize you're ready for a total overhaul. As you walk through your home room by room, ask yourself this simple question:

Do I love the items in this space?

It can be hard to edit what we have, because we think we must stick to our previous design choices—or even stick to our previous mistakes! If you read my book *The Gift of Home*, then you might recall I lived with a rug that was way too bold for our living room for over a year because I was too afraid to admit I'd made a mistake. And I was disappointed I'd invested in a trend that never truly suited me *or* my home.

I think back to the decor I had in our early years of marriage. It was the early 2000s, and black and red were all the rage. Sure enough, we had modern black furniture and black and red accessories all throughout our first apartment. While there's nothing wrong with those colors, they weren't ever reflective of my personal design style. Back then I didn't even know what my design style was, so I "borrowed" other people's styles and based my decor on that and what was trending.

When I began the journey of discovering my personal style, I noticed that none of the colors and furniture finishes I was drawn to were present in our home. So I began spray painting picture frames and candleholders white to reflect the aesthetic I was after. I refinished furniture to transform dark espresso stains into medium weathered-wood tones. I was both editing what was in my space *and* shopping my home to see what could be repurposed by making easy DIY changes or moving an object from a room where it wasn't a good fit into a space that would be refreshed by its addition.

These small, budget-friendly changes made a big difference over time. I remember noticing the shift in how I felt in our house. It became comfortable and familiar. When I returned from a busy day out or welcomed guests in, I felt immediate joy because my home finally made sense...my home felt like *home*.

Taking it room by room, identify what in your home needs to go or be moved to a different area. Do the colors and style of your accessories still represent what you love? What could be repurposed? Small, budget-friendly changes—if they're in keeping with your personal decor style—can make a world of difference!

MEANINGFUL STYLING

It's one thing to fill your home with decor, but it's an entirely different thing to be intentional about the accessories you choose.

CHOOSE MEANINGFUL ACCESSORIES

Accessories kick off the real decorating fun. These flexible, personal elements add character and interest to your home. While larger pieces such as furniture and area rugs can be our style stars, accessories are the supporting actresses that help tell our story and bring a space to life. It's one thing to fill your home with decor, but it's an entirely different thing to be intentional about the accessories you choose.

At this part of the decorating process, we are no longer trying to fit ourselves into the cookie-cutter version offered from big box stores. Instead, we're allowing ourselves to decorate with the purpose of adding meaning, not clutter.

Deciding on accessories can spark all the questions. *What do I include? What color should my accessories be? Are they all supposed to match?* To avoid feeling overwhelmed, I ask myself a few key questions:

Does this item reflect the design style I want?

Does it help incorporate a favorite color or pattern into the space?

Does this piece represent something in which I'm interested?

Does this accessory have sentimental or nostalgic value?

If you find yourself debating over which glass vase or throw pillow to buy, ask yourself this question: *Do I love it?* If the answer isn't a resounding *yes*, then hold out for something you truly love.

Look for pieces that incorporate your preferred patterns and colors and support the mood you desire. While I like for the overall look of my rooms to be neutral, I'm always on the hunt for accessories that incorporate my favorite colors, whether I find them in artwork, coffee table books, candles, throws, or tiny trinkets.

Accessories that introduce a different texture or finish into the space—like terra-cotta jars, shiny metal picture frames, and smooth marble bowls—can illuminate your style preference. Think relaxed versus elegant. Or rustic versus traditional. Those are just a few examples, but defining how you want the space to feel will help you make meaningful choices. Maybe you're an old soul but you don't have any family heirlooms to display. Incorporating found pieces from antique stores speaks to your love of history while the pieces share a story of their own.

Everyone has a different opinion about how many accessories you should have. Ultimately, you are decorating for yourself, so the right amount is up to you. Before I ever say a space is "finished" (I mean, is it *ever* really?), there are a few things I like to take inventory of. Did I fill every single surface and cover every square inch of my walls? Or is there some breathing room so the carefully chosen accessories can shine? Do I have too many similar items on repeat? While faux trees are great, I don't need one in every corner of my living room. Variation allows the uniqueness of each accessory to stand out. The goal is balance, not repetition.

Those tiny decor elements we keep collecting and adding for warmth and texture can soon overwhelm our homes and veer us away from our vision. When I find myself stuck in a decorating rut, I remove all the little decor pieces, bigger accessories with patterns, and even small furniture odds and ends from a space to create a clean slate. Often, only then am I able to see my space with a fresh vision.

Are you surrounded by so many small objects that you can't see the ultimate design anymore? Which of your rooms could use a refresh? Strip down the space, leaving only your anchor pieces. Now, pause to envision your design goal before slowly putting any items back. (Remember, some of them won't return to the space!)

BUILD A COLLECTION

My grandmother was a woman who loved building collections. She had them on display throughout her home, including ones for every season. As a kid, my favorites to sit and admire were the tiny houses and shops that made up villages and the tabletop Christmas trees that lit up when plugged in. She had so many collections that when the time came for her to downsize, she had a yard sale and the number one question people asked was, "Did you used to own a store?" I still laugh thinking about that day, but it also reminded me that somewhere between my grandma's generation and mine, people have talked themselves out of having collections.

While I would never encourage anyone to hold on to more than they need, I think we've lost sight of the value of collecting the things we love for fear of having too much clutter. As a result, we're missing out on those beautiful heirlooms that get passed down in a family...mementos that remind us of those who were here before us.

Consider building a collection of the things you love. Think of it as your personal signature. For each person, this is going to look a little different, of course, because we're all decorating with our own personal style in mind.

The homes that draw me in the most are the ones that have unique collections on display throughout their rooms. You don't have to fill every square inch of your home (or if you're like my grandmother, maybe you do). You'll want to leave some breathing room so that what you choose to put on display looks like it was curated with thoughtful precision.

I love antiques, but rather than fill my home with them, I choose to intentionally display only a few chosen pieces here and there. They are subtle reminders of a simpler time and balance out my beloved white accessories with their slightly worn patina. Take time to experiment with what you display, playing around with the amount and style that feels right to you. Your collection choice doesn't always have to make sense or stem from your family history. You might not be able to put into words why you love and are drawn to a certain item or theme, but that shouldn't stop you from making it a part of your home decor.

I have a love for antique European pickle jars. That probably sounds silly, right? I don't know why or even how this collection started, but I became enamored with these large recycled-glass jars. They are stately in size, somewhat similar to a demijohn bottle, but their wide mouth offers more versatility in their use. I always keep my eye out for them when I'm browsing antique stores. While the originals can be quite pricey, I sometimes find replicas in the kitchen storage section of my favorite home decor stores. While they're intended to hold dry pantry goods, I scoop them up, bring them home, and use them as vases for bouquets of freshly picked flowers.

A collection is something that is built over time, so don't feel discouraged if you're just starting out. Think of it as a scavenger hunt. You won't find all the items at the same time, and that is a good thing because the thrill is in stumbling across the perfect item, slowly building your collection over time.

What are you drawn to when you're out shopping or antiquing? What objects or groupings catch your attention when you're looking at photos online or visiting someone else's home? Can you showcase an heirloom collection from your family's history or start a legacy collection of your own to add meaning to your family's ongoing story? Some collections also come into being just because you like them. (I doubt my children will beg for my antique pickling jars to be a part of their inheritance!)

STYLING 101

Now that you've selected your accessories, and maybe even a few items to start a collection, you are ready to put things on display. You might be happy with your choices but unsure of how and where to place these gathered objects of affection. You might be asking yourself questions such as:

What should I group together?

How many items do I use in that grouping?

What if it doesn't match?

Are there any rules I should be following?

While these are all great questions to consider, sometimes they can lead us into decorating paralysis, causing us to stop before we've even gotten started. If questions like these are swirling around in your head, I want you to pause for a moment. Together, we're going to exhale those nagging questions and inhale reminders that we're doing this work to create a space we absolutely love. So, while rules are good, I prefer using *guidelines*—and allowing myself a heavy dose of grace along the way.

With any area I'm styling, whether it's a coffee table or open shelves, I keep a few guidelines in mind:

- Incorporate objects of varying heights.

- Arrangements in odd numbers are pleasing to the eye, but this doesn't always have to be the case.

- Items should fit the scale of the space you're arranging them in. Meaning, they shouldn't be too small or too big for the area you're working with.

◆ Try to incorporate different-sized objects. While some displays can be arranged with same-sized pieces—such as a collection of vintage bottles—creating smaller vignettes with objects of different shapes and sizes adds depth and creates layers in the visual display.

Don't be discouraged if your styling attempts fall flat the first time. Think of it as pursuing a creative practice. Often, when I'm building a vignette for my buffet or styling open shelves, I pause, take a step back, and evaluate my arrangement. I move pieces around or swap them out for different ones, scooting items back and forth until the spacing feels just right. Very rarely do I get it exactly right on the first try. By allowing myself the freedom to experiment, I've trained my eye to become more experienced in the art of styling, and you can too!

If you feel particularly stuck on a certain area, take a break. Walk away from it. Sometimes I like to leave the room and walk back into it later to see how it makes me feel. Other times I let something sit for a day (or two!) before I make up my mind about it. Don't fret! This is all part of the process of creating a home that feels meaningful to you.

Which room in your home needs the most styling help?
Walk into that room and do a quick scan of the area.
Which styled areas are pleasing to the eye?
Which feel cluttered or awkward? Based on your
observations, what small styling changes could
elevate the look and feel of the room?

my go-to styling staples

BOOKS | CANDLES | CANDLEHOLDERS | TINY SCULPTURES |
DECORATIVE LIDDED BOXES | JARS OR PITCHERS | FAUX POTTED
PLANTS | LAMPS | PICTURE FRAMES | SHALLOW BOWLS | TRAYS |
GLASS BOTTLES | FOUND OBJECTS | VASES

Terry John Woods' New Farmhouse Style

RECYCLE & REPURPOSE TREASURES

I am a bargain hunter. Some might call it being thrifty or resourceful, but for me it's all about loving the challenge of looking for ways to stretch my decorating dollars. While others might be discouraged about decorating on a tight budget, I get giddy with excitement when I find secondhand items I can repurpose or coveted decor items that have finally made their way to the clearance aisles.

Incorporating thrifted or vintage pieces can sometimes be the key to making your space less matchy-matchy and more one of a kind. There are several ways you can go about doing this, depending on your design taste and budget. While yard sales and thrift stores can offer you the most budget-friendly options, sometimes those one-of-a-kind treasures you're on the hunt for can take a little longer to find. If you are interested in authentic antiques, you might be able to find those more readily at antique stores or Etsy shops. Be prepared to do a little research first. The growing popularity of antiques can lead to a higher price, but if you find the missing piece you've been longing for, it can be worth the investment.

When furnishing a room, I like to balance out my pieces by mixing new and old together. In our living room we have a crisp white cotton sofa and gray linen armchairs. To balance out the clean lines of the sofa and chairs, I brought in a reclaimed wood coffee table and a smaller antique side table. I do this with my smaller decor pieces as well—old books, antique jars, and weathered wood objects add balance when paired with shiny picture frames, new candles, or a vase of freshly picked flowers.

When I'm on the hunt for furniture that can be recycled or refinished, I check to see if a piece is structurally intact and not missing key parts. While hardware is easy enough to swap out, sometimes finding the right hinge or missing piece of wood from a drawer or cabinet can be more difficult. I also look at the overall style of the furniture and study its lines. The age and design era of the furniture will impact the overall look of your space. Even though furniture can look completely different with a fresh coat of paint, the original design can't usually be disguised. Furniture built in the late 1800s will have a Victorian flair to it—possibly ornate, intricate details and lines—while furniture built in the 1950s and '60s will have the trademark cleaner, simpler lines of mid-century modern design. There is no wrong style, only the style that suits your likes and preferences, which is your "right" style.

REFINISHING OR REFRESHING WITH PAINT

There are a few things I take into consideration when deciding how I'm going to refinish a piece. First, I identify whether the piece is made of solid wood or wood veneer. Solid wood allows you to sand it down to the raw wood and then refinish it in a new stain color. If the furniture is made with wood veneer or engineered materials such as particleboard, then my best option for refinishing it is with paint.

Something else I consider before pulling out my sander is if the furniture has any intricate details in the woodwork that would be difficult for my sander to reach, such as turned legs or delicate moldings on the trim or doors.

Sometimes simply adding a coat of paint is the quickest and most versatile option for your repurposed find. I have been known to paint and repaint everything from hutches and dressers to picture frames and vases whenever I'm in the mood to freshen up the look of my home or a certain room.

The type of surface you are painting will indicate the best type of paint for the job. For rougher surfaces or furniture, my go-to choices are chalk paint or mineral paint. They require little prep work, and most of the time all that's needed before you start is a wipe-down. For smaller objects that are metal or have shiny surfaces, spray paint will be your best bet. For larger projects, such as repainting cabinets or working on pieces with smooth surfaces, water-based enamel paint is my top choice for a more professional finish. There is a bit more prep work required with this, but I have learned not to skip over this step. The extra effort required in the beginning will be worth it in the end. This is also true when it comes to sealing furniture after refinishing it. For furniture that will be susceptible to water spills or high traffic areas, like a dining room table or nightstand, I go with a water-based poly in a matte sheen. This provides a non-shiny finish and a higher durability for the wear and tear of everyday use. For accent pieces that won't be used every day or aren't susceptible to water spills, a wax sealer is my favorite choice. Don't be intimidated by finishes; there are plenty of tutorials available online to help you figure out which one is right for your project.

While out thrifting or browsing the shelves at my local HomeGoods, I enjoy looking for items that are similar to the high-end items seen in designer homes. If the piece is similar in size and shape but not the ideal color or finish, no problem! A little creativity is all it takes to repurpose an item in a budget-friendly (and fun) way.

As you do a room-by-room walk-through of your house, which furniture pieces do you see that you might want to refresh and repurpose in some way? Is there an item you were ready to get rid of that you now see with new eyes and possibility? Are you now more inclined to try refinishing or repainting it?

my go-to supplies for refinishing and repainting

ORBITAL PALM SANDER | SANDPAPER IN DIFFERENT GRITS | 1½-INCH PURDY ANGULAR TRIM BRUSH | FROG TAPE PAINTER'S TAPE | WIRE CUTTERS | STAMPS + STAMP INK | FOAM BRUSHES | FURNITURE WAX | VARIETY OF STAINS—MY FAVORITE COLOR IS DRIFTWOOD BY MINWAX | POLYURETHANE SEALER | CHALK PAINT—MY FAVORITE COLOR IS HURRICANE BY COUNTRY CHIC | ACRYLIC PAINT | DROP CLOTH | PAINT ROLLERS + TRAY | CLEAN RAGS | TWINE | PICTURE WIRE | FLATHEAD + PHILLIPS SCREWDRIVER | HAMMER + NAILS | HOT GLUE GUN | WOOD FILLER | 3M SANDING BLOCK | PLASTIC BUCKETS FOR MIXING

CURATE DECOR FOR YOUR WALLS

Do you have a blank wall that leaves you stumped when you try to imagine what to put there to fill the void? Is it making the rest of your room feel unfinished? Perhaps you've painted your walls the most perfect color. You've refreshed your furniture and even brought in a few new accessories, but something is still missing. Or perhaps you know you need to hang something on your walls, but you aren't sure what. With plenty of options out there, it can be hard to know what to choose. Do you hang one large piece of artwork or a grouping of framed family photos or something else entirely?

To get yourself going, take a couple of things into consideration. First, where is the empty wall space you're wanting to decorate located? Is it behind a sofa? In a hallway? Second, how big is the wall space you are trying to cover? Evaluating location and size will help you to consider your options with more clarity. The following three main categories of wall decor will help you envision and select the best choice for your space, needs, and style.

ARTWORK

When choosing art, first determine what type of art you like. Do you like abstract paintings or serene landscapes? Botanical and vintage images or framed photographic art? Is there a quote or verse that has special meaning to you that could be hand-lettered or painted and framed?

Tip: *Perhaps you already have some type of artwork hanging on walls, but they still feel empty or plain. Sometimes the answer is not putting up more objects or swapping small pieces for bigger ones, but enhancing the walls themselves. Think about adding wallpaper or moldings to give warmth to a space instead of just hanging more artwork.*

The type of art you gravitate toward says a lot about your own design style. If you're still not sure, think about your favorite places to daydream about or visit. I love the beach and antiques, so vintage-inspired paintings of the ocean are a go-to choice for me. When looking for ready-made artwork to incorporate into a room, look for pieces in the right color that will complement the rest of the space. Artwork is a great way to echo and highlight your preferred color palette.

DECORATIVE OBJECTS

Don't be afraid to add decorative objects to your wall decor. Architectural salvage, hanging baskets, mirrors, and clocks are all great choices for turning a plain wall space into a visual offering while providing a different option to framed artwork or photos. Mixing up the type of art you hang on your walls will add interest and balance to the space. For example, wooden signs are a great way to display a favorite saying or a family value that also tells your story. Perhaps hanging something that wasn't originally intended to go on the walls—like a vintage pair of skis or an heirloom plate—is just the type of unexpected touch your space needs.

GALLERY WALL

A great way to fill a large wall space is to hang a grouping of frames, also known as a gallery wall. This can oftentimes be a more affordable option than purchasing a large piece of artwork. First, decide on the type of gallery wall you like. Do you like a uniform look, with all the same frames, or a collected, eclectic look with a variety of frame styles and materials? How you hang your frames also speaks to the design style you are drawn to. A grid or linear style, where all the frames are hung evenly spaced, gives a traditional look. Frames of various sizes and shapes hung in clusters or groupings that are not symmetrical provide a collected, less formal look and give you more flexibility for placement.

Some of the most common choices for a gallery wall are family photos, themed groupings of similar photos like sailboats, birds, and vintage botanical prints, or a mix of original artwork and portraits.

Which wall is calling out to you for something intentional? Which walls are overburdened by objects and in need of an edit? What kind of art, objects, or even messages will bring you and your family joy when you look at them again and again? Those will be your go-to pieces.

Gallery Wall

While plenty of people find gallery walls appealing, many are intimidated to give it a go. I think the biggest hesitation is because the displays look complicated and painfully precise. If this is why you've been holding back from trying, I have good news for you. There *is* a way to create a gallery wall that isn't rigid. In fact, this is the style I find most attractive. I've always been drawn to gallery walls that look like they've been collected and added to over time. I love mismatched frames that showcase a mix of artwork and photos.

Are you ready to finally put together your own gallery wall? Here's some guidance to help make it happen.

SUPPLIES

+ Your selection of frames
+ Tape measure
+ Depending on your walls, hang pictures with finish nails and a hammer, sheetrock screws and a drill, or Command strips.

DIRECTIONS

Step 1. Before the first nail is tapped into the wall, I recommend that you create a mock layout on the floor. This allows you to move frames around easily before you commit to hanging anything. This is especially helpful when working with different-sized frames to create an asymmetrical layout. Once the frames are placed in a layout you like on the floor, use a tape measure and measure the length of the frames from left to right to make sure the grouping of frames will fit in the space where you plan to hang them.

Step 2. Choose a starting point. When working within a certain length of wall space, determine where you would like the center of your gallery wall to be. If you're using one large piece of artwork in the middle as the focal point, hang that piece in the center first. If you're hanging a collection of different-sized frames, start on one end and work your way toward the other. Finding the center first helps make sure you have an even number of photos on both sides. Since I was hanging my gallery wall over a console table, I hung the bottom frame first to make sure it was at the desired height.

Step 3. Arrange your additional frames. Stagger the heights and placements of different-sized frames, but keep the distance between the frames the same when possible. You can achieve a great effect by placing smaller frames stacked vertically on top of larger frames and alternating your frames vertically and horizontally. For my own gallery wall, I started by placing my first frame on the bottom left of our console table. Then I hung a second frame on top and continued working my way across the wall from left to right.

If you're hanging your frames in an asymmetrical style, you have more flexibility with the placement. More *grace*, I like to say, than if you were aiming for a symmetrical grouping, which would need the same distance between each frame throughout the grouping. Be sure to take a step back and assess your gallery wall as you hang different frames to ensure you like the spacing. If a frame looks disconnected, try moving it a little closer to the others.

Most of the time the frames will cover any tiny holes made from adjusting your frames, so don't worry if you have to move a frame after you've hung it. If your picture frames don't cover the holes, drywall spackle is a quick fix to hide any visible holes, and no one will be the wiser.

GIVE YOURSELF
THE GIFT OF TIME

We want an heirloom-quality look, but we often don't have the patience to acquire elements over time. We feel the pressure to have it all finished in a day—an hour, even—hoping a quick trip to the store will take care of everything we need.

Creating a space you love shouldn't be rushed. Your desired decor vision won't be accomplished in the time it takes to watch your favorite thirty-minute home improvement show. Allowing yourself enough time to think through each design element, including colors, patterns, and even wood finishes, is necessary to achieving the look and style you want.

When we moved into our current home, I made a vow to take my time decorating. Knowing that we planned to live here for the next thirty years, I wanted to be deliberate about every stage this house went through as we transformed it into our own place. When we first moved in, I unpacked our essentials so our family could live without much disruption, but then I sat with the blank spaces for a while. I spent time in each room observing the little details and writing down ideas I had for each space. We aren't there yet, but giving myself the gift of time when it comes to making decisions has allowed me to enjoy the process and be pleased with what I see unfolding in each space.

If you find yourself either frozen with decision fatigue or wanting to rush the process, allow yourself a moment to pause. Take a break and give yourself some time to acknowledge all the progress you've achieved in making your home meaningful. Sometimes we just need to give ourselves a little breathing room to allow creativity to strike again. Ideas tend to stop coming for me when I'm overwhelmed with too many choices or have too much on my plate.

Take inventory of the season of life you're in, and give yourself grace if you find yourself in a particularly busy season. And give yourself a break from too much scrolling online. As inspiring as social media can be, it can also often lead to discontentment with our homes and even our circumstances. I refuse to let the comparison game rush me into making decorating decisions or give me feelings of discontentment or a lack of gratitude. An unnecessary sense of urgency to have things perfect or to keep up with influencers or trends will ultimately undermine your chance to create a home that is meaningful to you.

Small changes, however tiny they may feel, can make a big impact over time. Don't diminish progress. When you start to feel discouraged about your space, look back and see how far it has come.

What is one thing you could do today to embrace a slowly unfolding decor process? As you look at the progress you've already made, what specifically gives you confidence that you're transforming this space into one that feels like you?

Part 2

Celebrating the Seasons

I've lived in New England, a region known for having four distinct seasons, my entire life. As a kid, I remember feeling the excitement that filled the air when a new season would begin and reveal its unique beauty in nature. I've carried that joy with me ever since, and to this day I love to celebrate all the seasons in my home and my life.

Think about what delights you about each season. Does a bouquet of fresh tulips mark the coming of spring for you? Do you love the smell of cinnamon in the fall? What does nature look like in each season where you live? Go for a walk outside and take note of the sights and smells around you. Let that be your guide for how you celebrate the seasons inside your home. When we choose to draw decorating inspiration from nature, we receive fresh perspective all year long. Instead of feeling bogged down by too much decor, we can simply highlight what we love most about each time of the year.

SPRING

Similar to the beginning of every new year,
spring brings with it a fresh start.

WELCOME SPRING

Spring inspires as we watch the landscape around us begin to wake up. As new life is coming forth up out of the ground, in the trees and bushes all around us, it's no wonder I feel that way in my soul as well. New possibilities, new ideas, and a fresh sense of hope, all bursting forth from within, like daffodils popping up from the ground after the winter snow. I used to say that fall was my favorite season, but every time spring returns, more and more I am convinced that it's my favorite. Something about the warmer air, the longer days, the birds filling the air with song once again, and the glimpses of fresh new green everywhere refresh and rejuvenate me after a long winter.

Similar to the beginning of every new year, spring brings with it a fresh start. Inspired by the new life I see around me, I can't wait to breathe new life into my home as well. It's time to throw open those windows and allow the fresh breeze of new possibilities to fill my home.

I like to view spring as the season of "firsts." The first time you see buds on the trees. The first time you hear birds singing again. The first time you walk barefoot in the grass. The first time the sun doesn't set before 6 p.m. The first vegetables that pop up in the garden. These signs tell me it's time to usher spring into my home as well. Galvanized buckets get filled with clippings of flowering branches, and I swap out my winter candles, with scents like cranberry and cedar, for the spring aromas of lilac and lemon. Any remaining signs of winter are put away as spring-cleaning commences to make way for spring decor.

As you prepare to welcome spring into your home, think about the things you love most about this season of new life. Is it a certain spring bulb or fragrance? Perhaps it's a pastel color or a floral pattern. Now is my favorite time to bring the outdoors inside because flowering crab apple branches and tiny buds only appear this time of year. We have the opportunity to celebrate spring all season long by what we intentionally choose to bring into our homes. Let's embrace spring together.

REFRESH WITH COLOR

Since the majority of our winters are spent hunkered down indoors, I find myself itching to swap out heavy blankets and fuzzy throw pillows once the spring air hits. The cheerful sunlight that once again floods our home has me ready to shed my winter layers and embrace the warmer days ahead. One of my favorite ways to transition our home into the new season is by changing out our bed linens and swapping my throw pillow covers over to lighter textures and fabrics.

Before putting them back on the furniture, I like to wash all the living room slipcovers. I add a handful of baking soda and a few drops of lavender essential oil to the load to help remove any stubborn odors and add a fresh scent back into the room. Those extra throw blankets that were brought out in the fall get laundered and put neatly back away in my linen closet until they are needed again. Wool and chunky knit throw pillow covers get replaced with lighter colors and patterns to match the new season.

When it comes to decorating for spring, I let color be my guide. In every season I choose one color to be the consistent theme throughout our decor. I incorporate it in the accessories I use for styling, whether it be the color of book bindings or the knickknacks I add to my displays. Sometimes I will even swap out the artwork in a picture frame to help reflect the current season we are in. I like to shop my home and rotate through pieces I already have that reflect the colors that feel like spring to me. For example, I feature sage green and pale blue for the warmer months while moodier colors like brown and gray get brought out for the colder months.

When you think about transitioning your spaces into spring, focus more on bringing in what feels like spring to you and less on what retail stores say you need to have. Subtle changes made throughout your home can make a big impact on the overall feeling you get when walking from room to room. Take note of any surface or area where you would like to add spring touches. You don't have to completely redecorate every room; rather, you can make some simple changes that allow you to refresh your home and highlight spring in a way that feels meaningful to you.

SHOP YOUR HOME FIRST

Look around your home and assess your everyday decor pieces. Depending on their color or finish, they might feel more like spring and summer or have more of a fall and winter feel. Would any of the pieces work for multiple seasons? What colors are your candlesticks, vases, and trays? Do you have lightweight throw blankets or pillow covers that you can use during the warmer months? While I don't believe you need to have a full inventory of decor for each particular season, I do believe in investing in pieces that will help you transition from colder months to warmer months. Get specific about what some of your decorating needs might be so that you can be intentional with what you buy.

---

spring decor staples

FERNS | SUCCULENTS | POTTED PLANTS | FLOWERING BRANCHES | LIGHT RATTAN TRAYS | BUD VASES | GLASS CLOCHES | TERRA-COTTA POTS | STRIPED FABRICS | MOSS

GATHERED GREENERY

You may have heard the term *vignette* before in the decorating world. I like to define it as "a grouping of decorative objects artfully displayed." In our everyday decorating, we do this to showcase what we love on side tables and bookcases, open shelves and coffee tables. When we do this seasonally, it offers us a chance to decorate with things we wouldn't normally leave out all year long, while highlighting what we love most about that season. One of the areas I do this in is the buffet in our dining room. As we go throughout the seasons in this book, I will show you how I create a vignette for every season on our buffet.

For me, springtime is all about adding greenery. In nature, greenery is popping up all around us, and I love to incorporate that same feeling inside our home as well. To begin creating my vignette, I choose a focal point. A large woven hanging basket tacked up on the wall and filled with spring branches sets the tone for this scene. Using a hanging basket in lieu of artwork or a mirror for a focal point is a great way to add a seasonal touch while also adding balance if the other walls in the room are already filled with flat objects like artwork or mirrors.

Every March I buy a few new houseplants to celebrate the coming season. They help tide me over until I can get back outside and tend to the plants in our garden. I use pots in different shapes and sizes to vary the heights of my plants. Little stands and pedestals are also used to add height if the perfect-sized pot isn't quite as tall as it needs to be. Lidded boxes and stacked books also function as risers and help in staggering heights.

I hunt through my coffee table book collection and sometimes my stash of cookbooks, looking for colors that will complement my spring color palette. I start by stacking books together in odd numbers, then placing them around my potted plants. I fill in the gaps with smaller cement pots and any other accents that speak "garden" to me. Working on either side of my hanging basket, I create two groupings of my decorative finds in odd numbers. (This doesn't always have to be the case, but grouping items together in odd numbers is a great starting point.)

Then I edit my vignette. I almost never end up using all the same items I started out with. And that's okay! Sometimes I remove an item or two if it feels too cluttered, or I add something else if it feels too sparse. When I was first starting out, I used to think this meant I was doing something wrong. But after years of tweaking and trying out different styling methods, I came to realize that this was just part of the process, not a sign of failure. If you are new to the process of creating vignettes, give yourself permission to play. Don't be afraid to shift things around, scooting items closer together or farther apart until it looks right to you.

Versatile Hanging Basket

I love the ease of gathering together a few faux stems and tucking them into a hanging basket. If making your own wreath feels too daunting, you are going to love the simplicity and ease of this DIY. Whether you hang it on your front door, above a mantel, or on your wall (like I did!), it will add big impact to any space with very little effort. The flowers and greenery you choose are entirely up to you, but that's what is so great about this project. You can reuse the basket season after season, simply swapping out the greenery.

SUPPLIES

+ Dry floral foam
+ Hanging basket
+ 1 to 3 branchlike stems
+ 2 to 3 faux greenery stems

+ 2 to 3 flowering faux stems, cut into separate pieces
+ Wire cutters (optional)
+ (Note: The size of your basket will determine how many stems you need.)

DIRECTIONS

Step 1. Cut the floral foam to size and place it in the bottom half of the hanging basket.

Step 2. Start placing branchlike stems toward the back of the basket, evenly spacing them out and securing them in the foam.

Step 3. Fill in between the branchlike stems with faux greenery, securing it in the foam.

Step 4. Cut the flowering stems into single branches instead of grouping them together. This will make it easier to place them in your hanging basket.

Step 5. Insert single flowering stems toward the front of the basket, spacing them evenly throughout the entire basket. Once you are finished, step back to ensure the stems feel evenly placed, and there are no gaps between the branches.

Refinished Buffet

To this day, I still remember the first piece of furniture I took an electric sander to. It was during our first year of marriage, and we were on a shoestring budget. Determined to make our first apartment feel a little homier, I spent the better half of a weekend refinishing a free-to-me coffee table with zero experience. The outcome was not my best, but I was hooked! For little to no money, I was able to transform a piece of furniture and give it a look that suited our style. This has become one of my favorite—and most resourceful—hobbies. We still own many of the pieces I've refinished, and some are now being used in other people's homes. If sanding down furniture intimidates you, don't worry! If I could encourage you with one piece of advice, it would be to *start small*. Find secondhand pieces that cost little to no money to practice on. Inevitably, there is always a moment mid-sanding when I ask myself, *What did I get myself into?* Yet with each piece I finish, I'm always filled with pride at not only the outcome, but the money I've saved as well. Below are the steps I take when I'm refinishing a piece of furniture, including how I refinished the antique buffet in our dining room.

SUPPLIES

+ Mineral spirits
+ Power sander
+ 80-grit sandpaper
+ 120-grit sandpaper
+ Sanding block
+ Tack cloth
+ Stain of choice (I used Driftwood by Minwax and Sunbleached by Varathane)
+ 220-grit sandpaper
+ 400-grit sandpaper
+ Furniture wax

DIRECTIONS

Step 1. Before sanding, take off the doors and the drawers and remove any hardware and hinges to ensure a smooth surface area to sand. Wipe down the piece and clean off any residue or gunk using mineral spirits. (Depending on the condition of the existing finish, some furniture may need to be stripped first—typically, furniture that is painted or has a glossy varnish. This can be easily determined once you begin sanding and find that the existing finish is not easy to remove. If you're unsure, you can always try sanding a small area first to determine if this step will be needed.)

Step 2. Using a power sander, begin sanding larger surface areas along the grain of the wood, starting with an 80-grit sandpaper. Once it's completely sanded, you will then want to run the sander over your piece of furniture again using a 120-grit sandpaper to remove any marks left by the 80-grit sandpaper. Use a sanding block to get into the corners and hard-to-reach areas. When finished, wipe the piece down with a tack cloth to remove all dust.

Tip: If there are any repairs that need to be done, now is the time to do it. Use wood filler or wood glue to repair any joints or chipped pieces that need to be fixed.

Step 3. Apply your desired stain color. For my buffet, I applied one coat of Driftwood by Minwax. Allow the stain to dry completely before applying a second coat or layering on a different color. (If there are too many inconsistencies in the color of the wood once it has been sanded, painting your piece of furniture will be the best option, as stain tends to emphasize imperfections.)

Step 4. Once your first coat of stain is dry, lightly sand the piece using a 220-grit sandpaper. This helps prepare the surface for the second coat of stain. Next, apply a thin layer of fast-dry interior wood stain (I used Sunbleached by Varathane), leaving it on for about thirty seconds, and then gently rubbing it in and wiping off any excess. Once you have covered the entire surface of the furniture, allow it to completely dry before applying your finish.

Step 5. Once your furniture piece has completely dried, lightly sand it with 400-grit sandpaper. Using this grit should only slightly buff your furniture without removing any of the stain, leaving the wood buttery soft.

Step 6. Using a clean cloth, apply a clear furniture wax. (Annie Sloan clear furniture wax is my favorite, but Minwax is a close second and can be found at most hardware stores.) Use a nickel-sized portion at a time and rub on thin layers using a circular motion. It should feel dry to the touch as soon as you're done. If you applied too much, it will feel tacky, and you'll need to continue wiping it until all the excess is off. Furniture wax takes thirty days to fully cure, so just be aware of that and don't have any water around it in the meantime.

{STEMS}

QUICK POPS OF SUBTLE COLOR

One of my favorite ways to welcome spring into our home is by adding pops of green everywhere. Without fail, come the end of February, I start to get the itch for spring. Feeling well rested after a long winter spent indoors, I love to freshen up the inside of my home by adding signs of life back into our common spaces. And I'm more than ready to throw open the windows and welcome in the fresh spring air as I add flowers and greenery to our decor.

Here in New England, it can feel like you're waiting an eternity for spring to finally arrive. Even if nature outside takes a while to get on board, with each passing day the calendar reassures me that spring is coming closer. When the trees outside aren't quite blooming, I look to my realistic faux stems to help me transition from winter into spring. While I always prefer the real thing, investing in some high-quality, realistic faux greenery is helpful for the in-between stage of the winter-to-spring transition. I look for stems that are made of rubber or latex, as these tend to look and feel more realistic.

Once late February hits and it's time to transition our home from winter to spring, I focus on removing any last remaining winter decor. I put away the last of the pine cones and cedar branches, swapping them out for moss-filled pots and flowering branches. Sometimes I do this all at once. And sometimes just putting away any remaining signs of winter and giving my surfaces a good cleaning is all the refreshing my home needs. Instead of being tempted to go overboard with spring stems (which social media can tempt me to do), I focus on areas where I can add a simple touch that makes a statement. When I'm debating whether or not to purchase faux stems to help get me through those in-between weeks, I ask myself if they can be used for more than one season: *Would these work for spring and summer? Could I leave these out from February to August?* When it comes to faux greenery, I'm not looking to have a full inventory for each season but rather a few pieces that will add a simple touch to my seasonal decor.

Spring stems don't have to be limited to just flowering branches. While I patiently wait for the ground to thaw outdoors, I like to fill smaller pots with spring bulbs and herbs for my garden. All winter long, I dream of the days when I can dig my hands into the dirt again. Getting an herb garden underway indoors allows me to get a jump start on my summer planting, while also adding some much-needed greenery back into our home.

Tip: *Potted herbs or spring bulbs placed in a row down the center of your table are a fun way to create an effortless centerpiece for your next spring gathering!*

DINING ALFRESCO ONCE AGAIN

One of my main motivating factors in getting our porch ready before the spring weather hits is being able to dine outside. I don't know why dining alfresco feels more exciting, but it just does! Here in New England, our outdoor dining season is shorter, so we take every chance we get to enjoy a meal outdoors. The moment the patios open up at our favorite local restaurants, you can bet our answer will always be "outside" when we're asked where we prefer to sit. You can bring that outdoor dining feeling home too. Have you ever noticed your family is more excited to help set the table if you're eating outside? Even if you don't have an outdoor dining set, a tablecloth or quilt can disguise even the humblest of tables. Spring offers us multiple occasions to gather and dine outdoors, so whether you are hosting a baby shower, Mother's Day brunch, or even Easter dinner, try adding some garden-themed details to celebrate the arrival of spring. (And remember: spring weather can be notoriously unpredictable, so it's always good to have a backup plan to move your party indoors!)

TEXTURED LAYERS

To lay the foundation for this spring gathering, I often reach for a quilt in lieu of a tablecloth. A cheery white-and-green paisley print matches the season and adds a touch of elegance if it reaches to the floor. Think outside the box and look through your linen closet for creative options if you want to switch up your look but don't have multiple tablecloths to choose from. Flat sheets, throw blankets, and even curtain panels offer us different options when it comes to adding layers to our table. To create additional layers, I use woven placemats for each place setting and fluted glass tea lights to incorporate different textures throughout the table.

GARDEN CENTERPIECE

Spring is all about new growth. To create a centerpiece that reminds me of one of my favorite springtime activities—gardening—I used three different vessels, in different sizes, to add variation to my centerpiece. You can use potted herbs, smaller house plants, or a mix of both to create a fuss-free option for adding greenery without taking the extra time to create a floral arrangement from scratch.

PLACE SETTINGS

I like to use classic white plates stacked with white linen napkins to keep things simple so the natural textures and other elements on the table stand out. To save space, gather each place setting's silverware together and tie it with a ribbon. Set the gathered silverware on top of each place setting.

Instant Cheer Floral Arrangement

It's no secret that I love flowers. Inevitably, a fresh bouquet of blooms always ends up finding its way into my shopping cart when I'm making my weekly trip to the grocery store. They add instant cheer to any space and always bring a smile to my face when I walk into a room. Over the years I've stretched my skills in learning the art of floral arranging, and I've discovered some helpful tricks for arranging flowers in an easy way that still makes a big impact. As we move through the seasons I'll share some of the more advanced floral arrangement techniques I've learned, but if you're like me and love a good hack every now and then, you will love the simplicity of this spring floral arrangement. The trick is actually not *how* you arrange the flowers; it's *what* you arrange them in. When I'm short on time but still want to create a beautiful arrangement, I start by choosing two vases of the same shape and style—but in different heights. By choosing two vases, you get the look of a large arrangement with the trick being in the heights. I've used this hack multiple times on my kitchen island, as a centerpiece for my table, and even on buffet tables when we are hosting large crowds. You can make this arrangement with your favorite flowers, clipped branches, or even a mixed bouquet from the grocery store.

SUPPLIES

+ 2 matching vases or pitchers in different heights
+ 2 to 3 bunches of flowers (your choice)
+ Pruning shears

DIRECTIONS

Step 1. Measure and cut the stems. Before you begin arranging the flowers, place one of the vases at the edge of the table. Next, hold up your stems next to the vase, lining up where you think you want the height of each flower to be in the vase. Then, cut off the bottom of the stem diagonally and remove any leaves that would be sitting in the water. Place the stem directly into the vase filled with water and repeat this step until both of the vases are full. Doing this for each stem allows you to measure, cut, and trim your stems to just the right height. Nobody likes bangs that are cut too short, and lining your flower up next to your vase at eye level ensures you won't cut them too short. If you do happen to make a cut that is too short, simply use that stem in the shorter of the two vases, or place it in a bud vase and display it on your bathroom vanity or kitchen windowsill.

Step 2. Determine where to place your arrangement. Once all your flowers have been measured, cut, and placed in water in the vases, it's time to display your arrangement. You can use this flower arrangement for a special occasion or simply because it's a Monday. It's totally up to you! Place the flowers where you are most likely to see them often, such as on your kitchen island or on a console table in your living room. I like to put the taller vase in the back and the shorter vase slightly in front of it, off to one side. This creates a subtle layer between the vases and keeps the flowers closer together, making a bigger impact in your space.

---

favorite stems and blooms

TULIPS | FERNS | PEONIES | LILACS | SEEDED EUCALYPTUS | CHERRY BLOSSOM BRANCHES | MATRICARIA | VIBURNUM | RANUNCULUS | HYACINTH

THE PERFECT FOCAL POINT

Our fireplace sits between our kitchen and dining room, creating a cozy spot in an otherwise open space. It is the first thing you see when you walk into this area of our home, which is why I like to decorate it to celebrate the season we're in. Whether you have an actual fireplace mantel or not, you can create a similar look by choosing a focal point in your space. In our previous home, I styled the buffet in our dining room as our "mantel." In your home it might be the top of a TV cabinet or a small table in your entryway. I use the same principles as I do when styling vignettes around our home, keeping in mind the size of my mantel.

I start by choosing a focal point that, to me, represents the season we are in. I hung two framed botanical fern art prints, side by side, as the center of attention for my spring mantel. The artwork visually represents one of the things I love most about spring—plants! The muted shade of green used in the artwork coordinates with the shades of green I like to decorate the rest of my home with for spring.

Once I have decided on my focal point and chosen its placement, I begin to shop my home for other accessories that I think will help me achieve the seasonal look I'm envisioning. I usually walk around with a basket in hand, placing objects inside that have colors and textures that I think

would work well on my mantel. This way, when I'm working on styling the space, I have multiple objects to choose from. I start with the pieces I think will work best, then swap them around until I'm happy with the height and placement. Doing this helps me to quickly identify the different shapes and sizes that look best. I often style a few pieces together, then take a step back to see how the arrangement feels. Nothing is off-limits until the mantel is complete. Like me, you might be surprised at just what you end up using to get your completed look.

Since adding in green for spring is my main focus, I like to group together different-sized faux plants. These add texture and variety. Some are potted and some cascade over our mantel. To add balance, I bring in some smaller books and vases that coordinate with the colors in the artwork. When looking for accessories to incorporate, focus on pieces that have a common thread with the overall theme. Since plants were the main focus of the theme for my spring mantel, I brought in a smaller glass watering can and a pin frog typically used in floral arranging for my final touches. Shopping my home first allows me to try out different options, helping me identify what I need to buy—if anything at all—to complete my display.

SPECIAL TOUCHES FROM NATURE

The hutch in our dining room serves as one of the main focal points in this space. Placed along a large wall at the head of our table, this larger piece of furniture helps ground our dining room, and the open shelves offer a place where I can display some of my favorite serving pieces. Given its size and stature in the space, it's the perfect spot to add some seasonal touches. It's where I begin my Christmas decorating, as the cubby-like shelves provide me a small, focused area to decorate. Come spring I'm ready to freshen up our hutch and add some spring touches throughout, which ends up impacting how the rest of the room feels. If you don't have a hutch or a large piece of furniture, look at other focal points around your space where seasonal touches might be added, such as a bookshelf or some floating shelves. You'd be surprised at what a little seasonal decorating can do to enhance the mood of the entire room.

To start, I begin by removing everything that is on display in the hutch. I wipe down all the shelves. After all, spring-cleaning is in full swing, and by this time of the year, the shelves are begging to be rid of their dust bunnies. I even take this opportunity to wipe down and clean any of my serving pieces that haven't been used in a while before placing them back in the hutch.

I start by placing my larger serving pieces in the hutch first. I fill up the top left- and right-side corners, then the bottom left- and right-side corners. I use my biggest pieces first, which makes it easy to fill in the remaining spaces with my smaller serveware. Using my larger pieces first in each corner will also help the overall look of my display feel more balanced. If you only have two large pieces, start with those and place them diagonally across from each other. Then proceed with your next largest piece, placing it in a diagonal on the opposite side. I use cake stands to add height, and I also stack coffee mugs and plates to help build height where I need it.

With my main pieces back in place, it's time to add in some spring. I take cues from my favorite springtime stems to determine what to add that will feel like spring to me. Potted ferns, tiny clay pots, and moss all announce that spring is in the air. Lighter-colored napkins and napkin rings add texture and balance out shiny white porcelain pitchers. I like to use what I already have on hand for springtime gatherings, choosing intentionally to put them out on display. These pieces don't have to be reserved just for special events. Hard-boiled egg cups say spring to me without feeling overly Easter. While I love to use my favorite serving platter and trays, sprinkling in a few special touches like bunnies and birds' nests is a fun way to display spring all season long.

Make-Ahead Curb Appeal Planter

During the first warm days of spring, I can't wait to get outside and bathe in the warmth. Just feeling the sun on my face and smelling the fresh air revitalizes my soul. I can't wait to give our outdoor spaces a refresh once winter is behind us, and that typically means freshening up our curb appeal. This planter is fun to make because you can start it in the fall. Once the spring temperatures start to get close to 50 degrees, I bring these previously planted containers out from where they've been stored in our barn and stagger them down our front porch steps. Here's what you need to create this spring planter:

SUPPLIES

+ Container / planter of choice
+ Potting soil
+ Fertilizer
+ 1 bag of spring bulbs per 1 to 2 containers (depending on container size)

DIRECTIONS

Step 1. Begin by filling your container with at least 2 inches of potting soil. Sprinkle a little fertilizer on top of the soil.

Step 2. Place bulbs pointy side up in the soil, ½ inch to 1 inch apart. Begin by placing the first bulb in the center, and work your way out from the middle of the container.

Step 3. Top with 4 to 6 inches of potting soil and water until the soil is damp.

There are a few factors to take into consideration when it comes to storing your containers over the winter. Depending on your climate, you will want to assemble your planters when outside temperatures are around 50 degrees. Containers can be stored outside if winter temperatures do not get below 35 degrees, and containers made of plastic are less likely to crack and break from water freezing inside them during the winter. If you're using terra-cotta containers or pots made of stone, you can store them in an unheated garage or shed. If you live in a cooler climate where your winter temperatures dip below 35 degrees, store the pots in an unheated garage or shed to protect the bulbs from freezing. Cover them with chicken wire or ground fabric to deter mice and squirrels from eating the bulbs. Water the pots every two to three weeks, keeping the soil damp. If the containers are stored outdoors all winter, keep an eye on how much rain and snow you accumulate, as you might not need to water them as often. Once you start seeing shoots poke through the soil in the spring, uncover and move your containers outdoors into your desired spots.

THE MOMENTUM OF SPRING-CLEANING

*If we had no winter, spring would
not be so pleasant.*

ANNE BRADSTREET

As soon as the weather begins to shift and winter's chill begins to melt away, you will likely find me completely submerged in a project outdoors. Whether I'm getting our outdoor spaces ready for use once again or working in the garden, I have an extra pep in my step as I dive headfirst into springtime tasks.

Of course, there is always the inevitable spring-cleaning to-do list that helps me usher in this new season. It's as though I can hear the house telling me, "It's time for a refresh!" Linens get laundered and rugs get shaken out. Windows and doors get washed. I scrub down our porches and pull our outdoor furniture out of storage to clean it as well. Everything gets cleaned from the inside out to help us invite spring in—and I always splurge on a new welcome mat for the front door. Those first 60-degree days have us ready to enjoy our outdoor spaces again, but if you have a heavy pollen season, wait until after the pollen mostly dissipates to bring out your extra cushions and throw pillows (unless they can easily be hosed off).

I like to take the momentum of spring-cleaning and use it to help me sort through closets and drawers, purging any items I no longer want or need. It always feels good to clean out any clutter that has piled up over the winter. I'm never motivated to tackle this chore once the summer season is upon us, so spring is when I go through our clothes, sorting through items that no longer fit or haven't been worn in a while and donating what doesn't work anymore. It feels so good to give all our spaces a refresh, including our wardrobes.

Spring awakens me from winter's hibernated state eager to soak up everything the season has to offer—taking in the fresh spring air on a walk outside or having a picnic lunch on our porch in the warm afternoon sun. I simply can't wait to enjoy the many sights and smells of the season. Like the chore list in every season, the spring to-do roster can sometimes overshadow the fun. To make meaningful memories this season, pick three things to enjoy as a family or with a friend. Maybe it's taking a drive to the city and enjoying the early blooms in the park. Or perhaps it's finding a new favorite flower to plant in your yard. Take time to sow seeds that will bring memories and meaning into your life and your home.

What three things would you like to enjoy this spring with family or friends?
What gets you excited about this season?

spring inspiration list

HOST A BRUNCH OR TEA PARTY | VISIT A GREENHOUSE |
CREATE A "DONATE PILE" AND DELIVER THE ITEMS TO YOUR
LOCAL CHARITY | PLANT AN HERB GARDEN | TRY A RECIPE
WITH FRESH SPRING INGREDIENTS | WASH EXTERIOR DOORS
AND WINDOWS | PURCHASE A NEW WELCOME MAT | LIGHT A
SPRING-SCENTED CANDLE | DISPLAY A BOUQUET OF TULIPS
OR DAFFODILS | POT SPRING BULBS | MAKE A SPRING CRAFT |
PLAN A GARDEN | TACKLE SPRING-CLEANING | HAVE FUN WITH
SIDEWALK CHALK | HOSE OFF YOUR OUTDOOR FURNITURE |
GET GARDEN TOOLS READY FOR THE SEASON (SHARPEN
BLADES, CHECK THE TIRE PRESSURE ON YOUR WHEELBARROW,
AND SO ON) | TACKLE A PROJECT AROUND THE HOUSE (MAYBE
GIVE YOUR FRONT DOOR A FRESH COAT OF PAINT) | SET UP
A POTTING STATION | CREATE AN OUTDOOR LIVING SPACE |
SPRUCE UP YOUR CURB APPEAL (TRY FRESHENING UP YOUR
GARDEN BEDS WITH NEW MULCH) | KEEP A JOURNAL OF
SPRINGTIME "FIRSTS"—FIRST BIRDSONG, FIRST BAREFOOT
WALK IN THE GRASS, FIRST LEAF BUD SIGHTING, AND SO
FORTH | WASH AND PUT AWAY HEAVIER BLANKETS, SWAPPING
THEM OUT FOR LIGHTER THROW BLANKETS | BRING SPRING
INTO THE HOUSE WITH SEASONAL THROW PILLOWS AND
SPRINGTIME FLORALS | WASH AND PUT AWAY YOUR WINTER
GEAR | GET OUT THE PORCH PILLOWS AND CUSHIONS

SUMMER

When we view summer as a season of delight, we can find fulfillment in the gifts we are given every day.

WELCOME SUMMER

Summer invites us to experience and enjoy life's simple pleasures. Flowers in full bloom filling the air with their sweet fragrance. The sound of busy bees collecting nectar. The smell of freshly cut grass. Favorite foods sizzling on the grill. Summer greets us with a relaxed atmosphere and a warm invitation to lighten our load.

Gone are the cold days of winter and the rain-filled days of spring that brought everything back to life again. Summer has a way of calling me to enjoy all things outdoors. Weeding in my garden or picking blueberries from our bushes. Spending an afternoon reading a book in a shady spot or taking day trips to the beach. Every day, summer offers us the opportunity to spend time nurturing and tending to the things that refresh our souls.

While the rest of my year is filled with schedules and routines, summer invites me to relax. With its carefree days, I instinctively feel the nudge to slow down and enjoy all the season has to offer. Since we try to spend most of our summer days outside, I tackle any remaining tasks that remain to be done *before* summer arrives so our outdoor living spaces are ready to use.

I stock up on all the items we use for summer entertaining—BBQ supplies; a full stash of marshmallows, chocolate, and graham crackers; and our favorite summer drinks. I walk around our home and put away anything we won't be using for the summer months. Baskets in our entryway that hold winter gloves and hats are now filled with beach towels and sunscreen, making it easier to head out the door on adventures.

I try to create the same laid-back atmosphere inside our home as well. I pare down the decor, putting away anything that distinctly reminds me of spring, and replace it with souvenirs that remind us of our favorite places we'd love to return. Keeping things simple inside our home allows us more time to partake in our favorite outdoor activities.

When preparing your home for summer, think about setting up your space in a way that will help you to enjoy the season rather than cause you more work. Consider paring down your decor for a simpler look. Or set up a hammock or umbrella to create a more functional—and fun—outdoor living space. You could even plan a staycation, where you intentionally abstain from all work and fill your days with play, creating the feel of a traditional vacation right at home. When we view summer as a season of delight, we can find fulfillment in the gifts we are given every day.

{TEXTILES & DECOR}

LIGHTEN UP YOUR LOOK

Summer is a season where I personally find refreshment, when school days and sports schedules are behind us and all that lies ahead are the carefree days of relaxing and enjoying a slower pace. I take time to set up our rooms in a way that encourages us to do just that! As the warm summer breeze blows throughout our home, I walk around and make simple tweaks to the decor in our spaces, acknowledging the subtle shift between spring and summer.

In our living room, I swap out throw pillow covers from soft neutrals to brighter shades of blue. Just like I use the color green in our home to signal the arrival of spring, I like to add pops of blue in the summer. It's a visual reminder to me of the sea, one of our favorite summer destinations, and coordinates with other accessories I use to highlight the season. I display tiny pops of blue in trinkets and artwork, and I swap out my spring-themed coffee table books to feature books with various shades of summer-blue bindings. Rotating a few smaller accessories in a color designated for that season is an inexpensive way to refresh your space without having to buy all-new decor.

Think about the colors that are already featured in your home. Since most of my decor is neutral, it's easy for me to seasonally highlight with a specific color. While I like to incorporate blues into my summer decorating style, that might not work with your color palette. If you prefer to accessorize with bolder colors such as red, then you might want to incorporate more creams and whites to lighten up your look in the summer. Swapping out some of your darker-colored throw pillows for accessories with lighter colors will help your space feel refreshed for the carefree summer months.

Don't forget about the textiles in your outdoor spaces! Summer months are meant for spending more time outdoors. Adding throw pillows for added comfort will make those spaces so much more inviting. Once summer is in full swing, I make sure that our outdoor living spaces are properly set up and ready for use. Here are a few questions I ask myself when I'm getting them ready:

How is my current seating situation working?

Do I have enough chairs for everyone?

Does anything need to be repaired or replaced before I put it out?

Do I need to replace any outdoor throw pillows?

Do I have any side tables I can bring out?

Are there any patio lights I can hang up?

(I highly recommend patio lights!)

---

summer decor staples

SEA GLASS | DRIFTWOOD | BEACH ROCKS | GLASS BEADED ROPES | CORAL CLUSTERS | WOODEN BOWLS | WHITE CERAMIC POTS | GINGHAM-PATTERNED FABRICS | STRAW HATS | WOODEN OARS

ARTWORK & ATMOSPHERE

In part 1, I shared how choosing artwork in a specific color is a great way to coordinate your decor and showcase more of your own personal style. This is also a technique I use to transition my decor to a new season. Artwork is a great way to share what we love visually, but we can also utilize the colors and scenes in a piece of artwork to tell the story of what season we're in. I keep a small inventory of season-specific artwork that allows me the flexibility to rotate the pieces throughout the year. Instead of incorporating a lot of seasonally specific decor, I let the artwork do the legwork of visually representing what season we're currently in, either with the colors used or the scene it depicts. You can see this in action in my summer vignette.

To create a focal point for my vignette, I start by layering two large, framed pieces of artwork. While large artwork can sometimes be costly, I created this DIY abstract canvas as an affordable way to fill some empty wall space. Placed in front of the canvas is a framed, vintage-inspired coral reef poster. The artwork in the poster depicts the atmosphere of the beach while also coordinating with my chosen color for the season: blue.

Next, I add in some height. Wooden candleholders, in a lighter finish for the summer, add height to both ends of my vignette. While I could have grouped all three candleholders together on the same side, I chose to break up the grouping by placing two candleholders to the left and one to the right. This provides variety while adding to the overall balance of the vignette.

Then, it's time to add in some seasonal greens. White cosmos gathered in ceramic vases are another visual reminder of the season and one of my favorite summertime delights. When considering adding in seasonal greens, look for stems that can incorporate your favorite flower. While flowers may only last a few days to a week, you can easily replace them with a different flower or foraged branches. That's the gift of summer—a never-ending supply of fresh greenery.

To complete my vignette, I add in a few more of my summer decor staples—recycled glass, white candles, a few collected beach rocks—to finish things off. Once you've identified which colors you want to incorporate for each season and which accessories speak of summer to you, you can have a clear strategy of what items you choose to decorate with for that season.

Take a look through the accessories you already have. Compile a list for each season, and then underneath write down the accessories that would best represent the colors and mood you want to see in that season. Automatically, some accessories will jump out at you and say "summer." Other accessories will work in any season. If you find that you have accessories that work for every season but one, then you may be lacking and you may want to invest in a few accessories for that particular season. Remember, though, the goal is not to have to go out and buy all-new decor for each season but to have accessories in the colors and finishes that represent the seasons to you.

Upcycled Vase

Every once in a while when I'm out window shopping, I stumble across an *almost*-right piece. You know, one that is the right size or shape, but the color is off. When I find something that is so close to being just the right piece, there are a few things I consider to determine if I can make it work. Can the piece be painted or refinished in a way that will fit with my decor? If the answer is yes and the price is right, then I quickly put the piece in my cart and run to the nearest cashier. That was certainly the case when I came across a terra-cotta vase that I loved. While stone pots and urns can be rather pricey in high-end stores, this medium-sized vase cost less than $20. The only problem was the color. Thankfully, I knew it was something that could easily be fixed with a coat of paint, and I could get a custom look at a fraction of the cost.

SUPPLIES

+ Vase
+ Newspaper or drop cloth
+ Lighter and darker paint colors of choice (2 to 3 different shades, depending on your desired look)
+ Paintbrush
+ Lint-free rag
+ Paper plate for dry-brushing effect

DIRECTIONS

Step 1. Place the vase on newspaper or a drop cloth. Paint the entire surface with 1 to 2 coats of dark-colored paint to ensure a complete coverage.

Step 2. Once the paint is completely dry, it's time to add dimension. To do this, brush on the lighter-colored paint in layers.

Step 3. Apply a small amount of the lighter-colored paint to the vase, rubbing it in with a damp rag. I suggest starting at the rim or base of the vase where natural weathering would occur. (Remember, if you mess up, you can always add more paint and start over.)

Step 4. Once the rim and base of the vase are done, add a few more dabs of the lighter color, gently rubbing it in with a damp rag and working your way around the vase in a few spots. The placement doesn't have to be exact, but the focus should be on adding layers.

Step 5. Once the paint is dry, use your paintbrush to apply a little more of the lighter color using a dry-brush technique. Dry-brush simply means putting a small amount of paint on the tip of your brush, wiping off the excess onto a paper plate, and lightly brushing it over the surface. This allows you to see the lines more clearly from the paintbrush bristles and adds texture.

Step 6. To finish, use the dark-colored paint to add your final layer, dabbing it in a few spots, and lightly rubbing it in where natural weathering would occur.

The hardest part of this DIY is getting started! At first, it might feel like you aren't doing it right, but layer by layer, your weathered vase will appear, revealing the perfect patina.

NATHAN TURNER'S AMERICAN STYLE

Pacific Natural   jenni kayne

BEAUTIFUL BLOOMS

If you were to ask me what my favorite thing to add to any space is, without hesitation I would tell you, "Flowers!" There is nothing I love more than grouping beautiful blooms together in vases or pitchers and placing them all around my home. Once summer hits, you will find me, clippers in hand, fully immersed in tending to our yard and the plants we grow around our house. I never used to consider myself much of a green thumb–type of person. I would flip through magazines and see beautiful gardens and think to myself, *I could never do that!* I thought people who planted gardens were just naturally gifted, or they came from a long line of gardeners.

Shortly after we moved into our first home, we needed to come up with a solution for a sloping portion of our yard. It was a section where our kids' balls always rolled down the hill and into our neighbor's yard, much to their dissatisfaction. Because of the size of the area and the inconvenient placement of the slope, installing a fence would have been a costly solution, one we didn't have the money for. So I took to the internet and did some research on what type of bushes, if any, we could plant that would mature fast enough to help provide some privacy and stop those dang balls from rolling down the hill. My research led me to Limelight hydrangeas. I'd always loved hydrangeas but was unfamiliar with this particular variety. I quickly found out that Limelights are hardy, sun to part-sun loving, and grow quickly, maturing at 6 to 8 feet. On top of that, they grew gorgeous football-sized blooms!

With a little bit of faith and a whole lot of courage, my husband and I proceeded to plant thirteen baby Limelight hydrangeas that summer. Each year, to our amazement, they tripled in size—with minimal effort on our part, I might add. For the first time in my life, I was able to cut flowers from my own backyard, something I had only dreamed of doing. I was hooked from that moment on.

Whether you have your own backyard with a flower garden or not, I'm here to encourage you to invest in planting a variety of flowers around your home. You don't have to be an expert gardener or have a lot of space. Begin with just one plant. You might be surprised at just how much you love it! Plant your favorite flower varieties, and you'll be gifted each summer with beautiful blossoms to cut and fill your home with. My favorite summer stems to decorate with are the ones I've planted in my own backyard.

Tip: *There are a few things to consider when looking for new plants to add. First, decide which area you want to plant in, taking note of how much sunlight it gets. That will be your starting point. Words I use when searching for new plants are "full sun" or "shade-loving." That way, I know which plants will work in the space where I want to plant them. Then I read up on them a little more. Are they drought-resistant or hardy to freezing temperatures? Figure out what zone you live in so you can choose your plants accordingly.*

Abstract Canvas

Neutral artwork is great when you want to fill up wall space but don't want something too busy or distracting. It's an easy way to add a pop of color, or a little bit of neutral texture when you want something simple in the background. This DIY works great on old artwork or a thrifted canvas.

SUPPLIES

+ Putty knife
+ Joint compound
+ 1 canvas
+ Paint colors of choice (acrylic, latex, or chalk paint)
+ Off-white paint
+ Paper plates for dry-brushing technique
+ Paintbrush or chip brush
+ Painter's tape
+ 1 × 2-inch pine boards for frame
+ Compound saw or hand saw
+ Stain of choice
+ Pin nails
+ Hammer

DIRECTIONS

Step 1. Using a putty knife, spread the joint compound onto the canvas in different directions. The goal here is to create texture, so don't be afraid about messing it up. You want to swirl the joint compound around, overlapping it, varying the coverage, with some areas being a little heavier than others. You can always go back and add layers once the joint compound dries; just be sure it doesn't go on too thick if you intend to paint multiple layers, as it will end up being too heavy on the canvas.

Step 2. Once the joint compound is completely dry, paint the entire canvas with the lightest color paint. For example, I brushed white paint on, leaving some raw edges of my canvas showing.

Step 3. To add a little depth, apply a tiny amount of off-white paint using a dry-brush technique and only applying it to certain areas of the white paint. You just want to add tiny layers with the paint, not completely cover the first color with the second color. Only highlight some of the texture and valleys the joint compound made. (Note: Dry-brush technique is when you dip the end of your paintbrush in a small amount of paint and then remove the excess, brushing it onto a paper plate or a newspaper, so you can then lightly apply a thin layer onto your canvas.)

Step 4. Using a darker paint color, paint one-third of the canvas to create a color-blocked effect. I used Wrought Iron by Benjamin Moore and painted the bottom third of my canvas. I made sure not to paint all the way to the edges in some parts (again, to create some texture). Using painter's tape to tape off the bottom section of your painting creates a smooth line. Or you can do what I did and use a chip brush, lightly applying the paint in a stamping technique so it appears more like a rough sketch and shows some of the brushstrokes.

Step 5. Once the paint is dry, assemble the frame. Measure each side of your canvas. While most canvases have equal sides, sometimes they can be slightly longer on one side. Always double-check your measurements first before cutting your wood. When measuring your canvas, remember that the vertical pieces of the frame will extend two inches past each side of the canvas in order to overlap with the horizontal pieces (or vice versa). When using 1 × 2-inch boards, this means you need to add four extra inches for each vertical length. Use a compound saw or hand saw to cut your pieces.

Step 6. Once the 1 × 2 pieces are cut, lightly sand any rough edges created by your saw, and stain the pieces in your desired color. I used Special Walnut by Minwax for my project.

Step 7. Once the stain is dry, using a flat surface, hold the first boards in place around the canvas and nail them in the corners, making sure to attach the boards to each other. Repeat this step for each corner until all four corners are secured.

EFFORTLESS ENTERTAINING

The summer months always feel like one big perpetual outdoor gathering. The doors to summertime open with Memorial Day and come to a close with Labor Day. With graduations, Father's Day, and the Fourth of July, there are so many reasons to gather during this season.

CENTERPIECE

A bouquet of freshly picked summer blooms commands a presence on the back porch table. Using a large serving bowl offers you a wide-mouth opening to fill the bowl with different flowers and stems gathered from the yard. The lightly colored woven seagrass adds natural texture in a material similar to that of wicker patio furniture that's so popular during this time of year. (See the tutorial for this arrangement on page 129.)

PLACE SETTINGS

Wood chargers lay the foundation for a casual summer place setting, especially paired with crisp white plates and blue salad bowls to incorporate favorite summertime colors. Woven napkin rings add texture while also tying in with the bowl used for the floral arrangement. Shatterproof acrylic glassware provides an elegant touch to this outdoor setting while white bistro flatware adds a relaxed feel.

DRINK STATION

When it comes to entertaining outdoors, one of my best pieces of advice is to set up a drink station. This alleviates much of the running around that can occur when we try to move our dining experience outside. Whether you fill a galvanized tin bucket with ice for bottled beverages or use glass decanters filled with infused water, having a drink station allows guests to fill and refill their cups, giving you one less thing to tend to.

{DIY}

Gathered Floral Arrangement

There is nothing I love more than walking around my yard with garden shears in hand, clipping flowers. I'm more of a bouquet-of-wildflowers rather than a dozen-red-roses kind of girl, and this summertime floral arrangement makes me feel like I just gathered them out in a meadow. Summer offers us the most beautiful array of flowers to choose from, so whether you are drawn to wildflowers like me or adore coordinated shades of pinks and purples, this simple arrangement is the perfect way to let the sweet aroma of summer fill your home.

SUPPLIES

+ 1 bowl or vessel
+ Floral or Scotch tape
+ 3 Limelight hydrangeas
+ 1 bunch of Lysimachia
+ Jasmine or vines
+ 1 bunch of chamomile daisies

DIRECTIONS

Step 1. Make a grid by fastening the tape across the opening of the vessel. You want the tape strips to be not much more than 1 inch apart.

Step 2. Measure and cut two Limelight hydrangea stems, about 4 to 6 inches, and the third hydrangea stem slightly longer (about 8 inches). Place the shorter hydrangeas on each side of the vessel. Then place the longer hydrangea stem next to one of the shorter stems.

Step 3. Cut two of the Lysimachia stems about 6 to 8 inches in length and place them next to the longer hydrangeas. Cut two more of the Lysimachia stems, about 6 inches, and place them next to the shorter hydrangea on the opposite side.

Step 4. Arrange some of the jasmine or vines around the groupings of flowers already placed in the bowl. I like to have one side drape slightly over my vessel, while on the opposite side I cut them longer so they stand outward more.

Step 5. Fill in the empty areas with chamomile daisies.

Step 6. Arrange some jasmine or vines around the edge of the bowl in a few places, allowing them to slightly hang over the edge.

---

favorite stems and blooms

HYDRANGEAS | SCABIOSA | SILVER DOLLAR EUCALYPTUS | COSMOS | CHAMOMILE DAISIES | ASTILBE | LYSIMACHIA | DOGWOOD BRANCHES | WHITE QUEEN ANNE'S LACE | CABBAGE ROSES

SEASIDE SOUVENIRS

Summer offers me the opportunity to put some of my favorite seaside treasures out on display. While I wouldn't consider my style totally beachy, in the summer it takes on a more coastal flair inspired by fond memories of spending countless days soaking in the sun up and down the New England coast. While I don't decorate with our found souvenirs from the beach all year long, summer is my favorite season to display them. They remind us of our favorite place to escape the summer heat, especially on the days we can't make it out there for a visit.

I display my collection of recycled glass bottles on the summer mantel. The smooth yet slightly imperfect details in the glass, with its slightly tinted blue color, reminds me of the sea glass we've found while walking on the beach. These bottles also make the perfect vessel for holding stems of snowball hydrangeas, a favorite seasonal statement. A summer activity our family enjoys is walking the coastline with the sand between our toes while we hunt for washed-up treasures. I always put out on display our finds of seashells, beach rocks, and driftwood we've collected over the years.

Hung above our mantel for the summer months is a framed painting of a merchant ship out at sea. The shades of blue used in the ocean and sky coordinate with the other blues I use throughout our home during the summer months, creating the perfect seaside backdrop.

When arranging my items on our mantel for the summer, I focus more on the overall balance of the grouping rather than the number of pieces used. You might remember I mentioned earlier that generally, grouping items together in odd numbers is pleasing to the eye, but that isn't always the case. I've grouped together four glass bottles on each side of my mantel, and I liked how that looked. Note that I *did* use different-sized glass bottles to incorporate different heights, but given the size of my mantel, adding in a fifth bottle felt too heavy, and only using three bottles made the display look too sparse. When deciding on how many items to incorporate, remember to take a step back and look at the overall composition of your styling. And keep in mind that not every surface you are styling is the same size, so there's always room for some variation.

PRETTY SERVING PIECES

I never used to consider myself a person who collected things. But over the past fifteen years, as my love for gatherings has grown, I've acquired a variety of different serving pieces to help fit my hosting needs. It's something I didn't even realize I was doing until only a few years ago. I'd collected pieces that were not only practical in use but also beautiful in appearance, and I couldn't bear to see them hidden away in cabinets or stored behind closed doors. I wanted to enjoy them all year round, so out on display they went!

While most of my pieces come from different places, they all carry a common theme. Sticking to mostly white gives me the flexibility to add to my collection over time (which my budget also thanks me for). Some of the pieces have unique details or patterns, but they are all carefully selected, giving my collection a curated look. Having my favorite serving pieces out on display means I get to admire my collection while also having it ready to use at a moment's notice.

The look of my hutch doesn't change much from spring to summer, but I do like to feature some of my favorite blue serving pieces and table linens in the summer. For instance, I like to display my hand-painted blue bowls and blue-and-white striped mugs that coordinate with the rest of my summer decor. Don't forget to incorporate table linens into your display too. Cloth napkins and favorite dish towels tucked into bowls or draped over a stack of plates add texture while softening the overall look. Some of my other favorite things to incorporate are silverware (antique is even better!) and napkin rings.

The pieces I've collected over time reflect my style and my love for hosting. One day, while I was adding a new piece to our hutch, I realized I had built a collection of the things I loved without even knowing it. Now, I look for special occasions—like a birthday or anniversary—to add pieces to my serveware collection. I also like to find items when I travel. For instance, I remember a special trip to a coastal town in Rhode Island every time I look at my white stoneware mugs.

Whether you have inherited heirloom hand-me-downs, love to buy artisan-made items, or enjoy hunting for vintage pieces to mix and match, take your time building a collection of pieces that communicate what is meaningful to you.

Mixed Medley Planter

When choosing plants for your summer planter, I like to keep a few things in mind. Always incorporate one plant that flowers. Use plants with different heights. And choose one cascading plant if possible. Sometimes, doing all three can be a challenge, but I love the variety it adds when you have a mixture of plants. I also like to look for plants that offer different textures. Lamb's ear has longer, oval-shaped leaves that are fuzzy to the touch, just like their name describes, and offers a silver shade of soft green that contrasts nicely against plants with darker green foliage. Stonecrop is great for its soft muted color; it has a waxy texture and can also be transplanted into the ground once the season is over. I also love incorporating herbs like rosemary and sage that offer a different texture from most plants—plus the added benefit that I can snip them all summer long for my cooking.

SUPPLIES

+ 1 planter
+ 1 bag of soil
+ White impatiens
+ Lamb's ear
+ Silver Falls (dichondra)

DIRECTIONS

Step 1. Fill your planter with soil.

Step 2. When using three plants, visually divide your planter circumference into thirds.

Step 3. Place the tallest plant into the soil first, then the next tallest plant, and so on. Think about where you will place your planter once it's completed. I typically place mine up against our house, so I make sure I arrange the planter so that my tallest plant will be placed in the back, and the shorter plants placed on either side so they can be seen from all angles.

Step 4. Once you've put all three plants in the container, fill in any remaining gaps with soil.

Step 5. Fully water the plants to encourage the roots to become established.

TAKE TIME FOR SIMPLE PLEASURES

Every summer like the roses, childhood returns.

MARTY RUBIN

Summer invites all of us to be kids again. As we grow older, it's easy to lose sight of the importance of play. Gone are the days when the bell would ring on the last day of school, signaling to us that summer was now in session. As adults, to-do lists pile up and schedules fill with the demands of work and family life. However, with a little bit of conscious effort, we can find ways to delight in summer all season long—and to play like the kids we once were.

Be intentional about carving out time that will allow you to enjoy summer's simple pleasures. Delight in the gift of abundance that comes in summer by visiting a farm stand or making a dish with fresh vegetables grown in your garden. If you're new to vegetable gardening, cherry tomatoes can be grown easily in a pot and taste oh-so-sweet right off the vine.

When my kids were little, setting up the sprinkler in our backyard would suffice for an afternoon of fun. But as they have grown older, so has our assortment of outdoor activities. Our entire family enjoys lawn games. Whether it's a kickball competition or stacking jumbo wooden blocks in the grass, there is something for everyone. No pool? No problem! Fill a large bucket with water balloons, and you've got yourself a competitive game of kids versus parents or boys versus girls. You choose! For our family, making summer meaningful always means setting aside time to play.

Even if your schedule is still busy in the summer, you can always enjoy the refreshment that comes when you take time to play and enjoy all the little things of the season. You also don't have to be limited by your circumstances; many activities can be done right at home. Set up an outdoor seating area, even if it's just a picnic blanket in a shady spot, and leave your phone inside. Relax and soak in what nature is doing around you. Invite neighbors over for a refreshing drink on your porch or patio. Go for a bike ride and allow the fresh breeze to revitalize your soul. Sit under the stars and count how many asterisms you can find. Grab a book and read in the shade or, better yet, take a nap! There are so many ways summer invites us to find refreshment; we need only grant ourselves permission to play.

How might your favorite childhood memories
of summer inspire you as an adult?

---

summer inspiration list

VISIT A FARMERS' MARKET | HOST A BARBECUE | TAKE A NAP ON THE PORCH OR IN A HAMMOCK | MAKE HOMEMADE POPSICLES | ENJOY A SLICE OF WATERMELON | GO FOR A HIKE | TAKE A TRIP TO THE LAKE OR OCEAN | PLAY LAWN GAMES | HAVE A PICNIC | ENJOY A CAMPFIRE | READ A BOOK UNDER A SHADY TREE | PLANT SOMETHING NEW IN YOUR YARD | ENJOY YOUR FAVORITE SUMMER RECIPE | FLOAT IN A POOL OR DOWN A RIVER | GO OUT FOR ICE CREAM | CREATE A BOUQUET WITH SUMMER FLOWERS | LIGHT A CANDLE IN YOUR FAVORITE SUMMER SCENT | CREATE A SUMMER PLAYLIST | FLY A KITE | GO TO AN OUTDOOR CONCERT | PLAY AT THE PARK | WATCH A MOVIE UNDER THE STARS | ATTEND A BASEBALL GAME | PAINT ROCKS FOR YOUR GARDEN OR WALKWAY | HIT UP A YARD SALE | HAVE A WATER BALLOON FIGHT

FALL

This is a season of comfort, and the return of crisp and cool air has us reaching for cozy blankets and sweaters to keep us warm.

WELCOME FALL

As much as I long for an eternal summer, I find myself ready with anticipation for the routine that returns in the fall. Lazy days are behind us and excitement fills the air as the kids head back to school. Farm stands fill up with pumpkins, and annual activities like apple picking and corn mazes return like old familiar friends.

As the days grow shorter, my attention turns back indoors, and I'm ready to welcome fall into our home. You will likely find me puttering around with a pumpkin spice coffee in hand while "Autumn Leaves" by Nat King Cole plays on repeat in the background. As I transition into the new season, I surround myself with sights and smells and sounds that speak "fall" to me. This is a season of comfort, and the return of crisp and cool air has us reaching for cozy blankets and sweaters to keep us warm. Savory aromas begin to fill the air with the return of slow-cooker meals and simmering stews on the stove.

Welcoming fall into our homes doesn't have to happen all in one day. In nature, fall arrives little by little as the leaves slowly turn color. I like to mimic nature's approach and take my time transitioning our home over to fall, focusing on one area at a time. This allows me to delight in autumn all season long instead of feeling the urgency of a chore that has to be done in a day. From swapping over my throw pillows and artwork to putting together a fall planter to spending an afternoon creating a simple fall vignette, each activity brings a subtle change that offers me a chance to savor all the season has to offer.

As you begin to transition your home from summer to fall, think about the colors and scents of autumn that speak to you. And remember to slow down and enjoy the process. Soak in all the comforts that fall brings. Welcoming a new season into your home isn't just about the decor either. What meals or warm drinks do you enjoy in the autumn? Do you have a favorite fall scent or candle? Create a fall playlist so you can enjoy not only the sights but also the smells and sounds of fall as well.

COZY & COMFORTABLE

Living in New England, we get the best showcase of all the beautiful autumn colors. And while I love the vibrant colors in nature that fall is known for, I don't necessarily love decorating with those colors inside my home. Fortunately, there are many different color options when it comes to fall decorating. To keep my home feeling cohesive through the seasons, I like to keep my fall decor in the same color palette. I'm drawn to the subtle colors of the season, such as muted shades of tans and greens. I also focus on incorporating textures and patterns, like plaids and flannels, into my decor instead of relying on traditional fall colors.

The crisp autumn air reminds me it's time to prepare for winter inside our home. Extra blankets get brought back out on beds after being tucked away for spring and summer. Chunky knit throws with soft, cozy textures get tucked into baskets so they're always at arm's reach. I swap out my throw pillow covers in the living room for hues that feel more like fall. Soft flannel and faux fur—nothing is off-limits when it comes to embracing fall throughout our home.

Fall is all about nesting, making our home feel warm and comfortable as we prepare for the colder months ahead spent indoors. I like to focus on all the senses when I'm welcoming fall. Candles get swapped out from scents like island margarita to harvest apple spice, and I light them more, enjoying their ambient glow as the days grow shorter. I take note of how each space in our home is being used and ask myself if anything needs to be moved around or reevaluated so our rooms can serve us properly for time spent indoors.

While I have nothing against traditional orange pumpkins, I personally am drawn to the more muted colors pumpkins can come in. Whether they are faux or real, I go for creams and muted green tones. My favorite approach to decorating for fall is simple: I believe in the power that a single pumpkin can make in a room. I simply walk around our home placing a pumpkin here and a pumpkin there—atop a stack of books, on the kitchen island, in the entryway. I also look for ways I can incorporate bits of fall into our artwork, displaying pictures of turkeys and pumpkins or a beautiful autumn scene. By swapping out artwork, I can easily welcome fall into our home without having to change up the placement of my picture frames. Let nature be your guide. Whether it's filling a vase with turkey feathers you found on a nature walk or setting out a basket of acorns that have fallen from the trees, using pieces that you've collected from nature allows you to decorate for fall simply yet timelessly.

fall decor staples

PUMPKINS | FLANNEL BLANKETS | PINE CONES | FALL FOLIAGE BRANCHES | WHEAT GRASS | COPPER PITCHERS | BRASS CANDLESTICKS | ACORNS | WINTER GOLD (ORANGE) | BERRY SPRAY | PHEASANT TAIL FEATHERS

{DIY}

Antique European Basket

When our kids were little, they shared a room. To help organize their toys, we purchased matching wicker trunks to place at the end of each bed. I took inspiration from antique European baskets that were stamped with the owner's initials and stenciled my children's birthdates across the middle of each of their trunks. This made each trunk personal for my kids, which was especially helpful when it came to putting their toys away in the correct place. It also added a bit of old-world charm to their space. The most common use for baskets in our home today is to hold all our throw blankets, but they can also be used for additional storage in any room or as a planter for a faux tree. Personalizing them by stamping them with your initials or a special date is a great way to add a bit of historic charm that's personal to you.

SUPPLIES

+ Basket of choice
+ Painter's tape
+ Black craft paint
+ Paper plate and sponge brush
+ Letter and number stencils

DIRECTIONS

Step 1. On your basket, determine where you would like to place your stenciled letters or numbers.

Step 2. Using painter's tape, tape off a border around the designated area you wish to stamp. This will help keep your letters and numbers in a straight line. It will also help you determine the spacing of each letter or number before stenciling it on with paint.

Step 3. Pour paint onto the paper plate and blot the sponge brush into the paint.

Step 4. Holding your stencil in place, begin to apply the paint with the sponge brush to the basket.

Step 5. Once the desired letters or numbers have been painted, allow your project to dry completely, then remove the painter's tape.

Step 6. You can also use painter's tape to paint stripes or add markings to your basket for a more authentic look.

A COHESIVE COLOR PALETTE

Years ago, when I was helping my mom create a Thanksgiving tablescape for her home, I found a white terra-cotta turkey while out shopping one day. I will never forget the startled look on the lady's face next to me as I gasped out loud upon laying eyes on this sweet little turkey. I can't remember if it was because I felt like I'd found the perfect missing piece to complete my mom's tablescape or because it was on sale. Either way, I knew it was coming home with me. Years later, I am still the proud owner of that turkey, but rather than save it just for Thanksgiving, I incorporate it into my fall decor so I can enjoy it all season long.

To create this fall vignette, I keep my DIY canvas painting in place from my summer vignette, but for the layer in front of the canvas, I replace the summer artwork with an old mirror. Doing this allows me to reuse pieces I already have in place while refreshing my focal point for the new season. Since most of my seasonal fall decor pieces are neutral, the pop of color from the canvas helps my white pumpkins stand out while adding some depth to my display.

I use pumpkins of all the same color for a more uniform look. I display different shapes and sizes throughout to add variation, which is especially important since they are the same color.

A large recycled glass jar holds a grouping of fall stems to add height to the rest of my fall decor pieces. I also add taper candlesticks and stacked books to elevate the smaller pumpkins. I like to create little groupings with staggered heights to keep the eye moving throughout the display. Turkey feathers tucked into a milk glass pedestal that has been filled with mini pine cones add height in an original and unexpected way.

Whether it's a console table, a coffee table, or a buffet, focus on your preferred color palette when you're choosing which items to display in your fall vignette. Autumn offers us a variety of shades and colors, but to maintain a cohesive look throughout your home, try to select items that incorporate the same colors. Since my home is mostly neutral, I set the tone for each season with the colors I choose to incorporate. If warm tones are your favorite, look for foliage that features orange and brown hues. Woven baskets and antique copper accents can play into your color palette while also adding in different textures. If cool tones are your favorite, look for muted green- and khaki-colored pumpkins. Ornamental kale and wheat grass will add natural texture to your cooler-toned color palette. Remember, there is no wrong color palette when it comes to fall—just the one that is right for you and your decorating style.

FORAGING OUTSIDE YOUR FRONT DOOR

I will never forget the first time I decorated our home for the fall. We had only been in the house for a few months, and I'd been bitten by the fall nesting bug. Completely submerged in setting up our new home, I was excited to decorate it just the way I wanted to. I'd picked up the latest issue of *Better Homes & Gardens*, and I was so inspired to decorate for autumn. The only problem was that there was zero money in our budget for me to go out and buy any fall decor. At first, I was disappointed as I thought to myself, *I'll just have to wait until next year.* But then I decided to get resourceful. I cut out pictures of pumpkins from the magazine, glued them to white cardstock, and placed them in picture frames I already had. I filled my vases with acorns the kids and I gathered from our walks in the woods, and I placed a simple white pillar candle in the center. I clipped branches from our yard with leaves that were changing color and arranged them in a galvanized bucket on my dining room table. I got crafty, foraging what I could. And it was okay that I didn't have money to go out and buy the latest in fall decor; our home "felt" like fall with the glowing candle I lit and the treasures from nature I'd collected.

Welcoming fall into your home doesn't have to cost a lot of money or require a ton of effort. Whether you go all out with your fall decor or like to keep things simple, the question you need to be asking yourself when decorating is, *Does this feel like fall to me?* Sometimes we can trick ourselves into thinking we need more decor in order for it to feel "done." This could be the case if you're just starting out, but I believe the best method for decorating is to let nature take the lead.

What does fall look like where you live? You may not reside in a region where the leaves are changing, but I can bet that if you stepped outside your front door, you could still see signs of fall. Welcoming fall into our homes doesn't have to look like a retail store display. When I'm ready to decorate for autumn, the first thing I like to do is go for a walk outside and see what I can forage. Sometimes it's branches, sometimes it's pine cones, and when I'm really lucky, sometimes it's a turkey feather or two!

There is something about taking a walk outside and looking at nature as though through a microscope as you search for treasures. Over the years, I've invested in some realistic-looking faux fall branches to help get me through the in-between times, when the leaves are no longer on the trees. I like to decorate with a mix of both faux and real to add longevity to my fall decor. Remember, you don't have to buy all-new—or all-faux—to decorate for fall. Decide what is most important to you, and go from there.

Tip: *You can keep foraged branches lasting longer by first cutting a 1-inch slit in the bottom of each branch to allow more water to be absorbed. Next, remove any lower leaves or greens so only the stems are in the water. Make sure you change the water every other day to keep the branches from rotting.*

PUMPKINS & PICNICS

One of my favorite things about fall in New England is the beautiful display we get courtesy of nature. Leaves begin changing at the end of August, and by the first week of October, they are on full display. I like to try and capture the subtle yet constant changes, so daily I step out into our backyard to savor the scenery, because I know all too well that the amazing colors and enjoyable temps are only here for a little while longer. I can't think of a better way to celebrate fall and all its beauty than by gathering outdoors.

CENTERPIECE

For this outdoor gathering, I don't want to compete with the beautiful fall backdrop already provided by nature, so rather than use flowers or branches for my centerpiece, I go with my second-favorite fall staple—pumpkins! I fill the center of my table with an assortment of pumpkins and squashes in different shapes and sizes. I start by placing the largest pumpkin in the center of the table. Next, I place the medium-sized pumpkins and squash closest to my large pumpkin in the middle, and then fill the display in with smaller white pumpkins and baby butternut squash, working my way out from the center.

PLACE SETTINGS

To help balance out the picnic-like feel of this gathering, I opt for nicer plates and flatware to create each place setting. I found a brown transferware set at HomeGoods years ago, and they are still my favorite to use in fall because of the color and antique feel. Pairing them with antique silverware adds a little bit of elegance to this rustic setting. I finish off each place setting with white linen napkins tied in a casual knot, with a pine cone adding a simple seasonal touch.

TERRIFIC TEXTURE

In lieu of a table cloth, I like to add texture by placing cozy throw blankets in various seats around the table. Gathering outdoors in the fall means cooler temperatures creeping in as the evening progresses. Having throw blankets handy ensures that no one has to leave the party early because they are too cold. I use some of my leftover pumpkins in clusters on the ground around the table to provide yet another texture and ground the table.

Tip: Having a plan to gather outside in the fall doesn't have to make you anxious. If the weather is clear, set up your table a day in advance to allow more time for preparation the day of the party. I fill crates and baskets inside with everything I plan to use (utensils, plates, table linens), which makes it easy for my kids to help me bring stuff out, and means I take fewer trips back and forth.

An Asymmetrical Floral Arrangement

This asymmetrical arrangement is easier to make than you would think. What makes it asymmetrical is that the stems on the right side are taller than the stems on the left side. When I have a little more time to play with my arrangement, this is my go-to choice. It has more of a whimsical feel to it than a traditional arrangement with flowers placed in a vase. Because it's asymmetrical, you don't have to worry about things being exactly the same height all around, which gives you more flexibility when assembling the arrangement.

SUPPLIES

+ Urn or shallow-footed vessel
+ Wet floral foam
+ 3 stems with large blooms (I used dried Limelight hydrangeas)
+ 4 to 5 light-colored flowers with medium-size blooms
+ 3 to 4 dark-colored flowers with medium-size blooms
+ Handful of Vegmo snowball stems or other small flowers
+ 2 foraged branches
+ 2 to 3 maidenhair grass stems
+ Handful of dried foliage

DIRECTIONS

Step 1. Begin by placing the wet floral foam in the base of your bowl. You can use a kitchen knife to cut the bricks so they fit securely in the bowl's base. Fill the bowl with water and allow the bricks to become completely soaked.

Step 2. Start by placing three of the largest flower stems into the foam at a 45-degree angle. You can cut one dried hydrangea stem shorter and place it closer to the rim on the left side of the urn. Then place two longer-stemmed hydrangeas at an angle on the right, staggering their heights. This creates a V-shape in the center of the arrangement.

Step 3. Fill in around your largest blooms with medium-sized flowers. Cut some to shorter lengths and some to longer lengths and place them off-center so they keep a V-shape in the arrangement.

Step 4. Fill in any gaps with the smallest flowers. For this step you can use Vegmo snowball stems, which look like tiny white buttons.

Step 5. Use foraged stems and branches, like maidenhair grass stems, to fill out both sides, accentuating the overall V-shape of your arrangement. To do this, place branches underneath the shorter-cut flowers so they cascade over the side of the urn. On the opposite side, cut branches at longer lengths to add more height, and place them in the floral foam, filling in around the dried hydrangeas.

Step 6. To finish, view the arrangement from all sides. Use leftover foliage to fill in any gaps where floral foam is still visible.

favorite stems and blooms

MAIDEN GRASS | KALE | DRIED PODS | CHOCOLATE QUEEN
ANNE'S LACE | DAHLIA | SEDUM | DRIED CATTAILS | GOLDEN
YARROW | RASPBERRY HYDRANGEA | THISTLE

THE WARMTH OF THE FIRESIDE

With fall comes the return of fireplaces and wood-stoves in the home. The familiar smell of burning wood, along with the infinite warmth it brings, is all the inspiration I need to get me in the mood to make the rest of our home feel cozy. When it comes to decorating our mantel for fall, I begin by thinking about what I want to use as a focal point. Will it be a mirror or a large piece of artwork showcasing a beautiful fall scene? Or perhaps a sign pointing to the nearest pumpkin patch? Whatever you decide on as your focal point, choose one that inspires you and reminds you of fall. Once I've settled on a focal point, I look to my seasonal decor staples to add interest and complete the overall look. Whether you like to re-create the same look year after year or switch things up, starting with your focal point and incorporating your seasonal staples will keep you on the right track.

To create my favorite look for my fall mantel, I start off by placing an old bread board layered with an antique silver serving tray in the center to create a focal point. The tray reminds me of one you would serve turkey on for Thanksgiving, offering a subtle nod to one of the season's best-loved holidays. Whether you use serving platters or a framed piece of artwork with a fall scene, think about what says "fall" to you. Knowing that I wanted to incorporate a smaller framed picture of a pheasant into my display, I chose neutral larger pieces as my focal point so they wouldn't compete with my framed print.

For height, I display brass candlesticks with tan taper candles on either end to add in the warm tones I love for fall. Placing the taller candlesticks closest to the platters on either side and the shorter candlesticks on the outside creates a semicircle shape above the mantel, giving me guidelines for my overall design.

Next, I add in some seasonal touches. These pieces really help bring my autumn mantel design to life. I place little clusters of mini white pumpkins and muted orange pumpkins around my candlesticks, then add some fall foliage. Clipped branches give the display texture, and I don't have to worry about keeping them in water, which is great if you're tight on space. To finish off my fall mantel decor, I tuck in a few turkey feathers and nestle some goldenberry clusters around the pumpkins, filling in any gaps or bare spots.

Thrifted Frame Makeover

I will admit it: I'm not an avid thrift-store shopper. While I love the amazing deals you can get there, antique stores will forever be my first choice. However, when I'm on the hunt for inexpensive frames, the thrift store is the place I look first. It's one of the best spots to find inexpensive frames and even artwork. However, what happens when you find a frame that's the perfect size you're looking for but the color and the artwork are off? You flip it! With a little bit of paint, you can breathe new life into those discarded frames. You've heard the saying "One man's trash is another man's treasure," right? I have definitely found that to be the case when it comes to thrift-store picture frames. There are many different methods for giving your thrifted frame a makeover. Spray paint, chalk paint, or even a little rub 'n buff can do the trick. The method you choose will depend on the finished look you desire, but here is one way I like to refresh frames.

SUPPLIES

+ Thrifted picture frame
+ Chalk paint
+ Printable artwork

DIRECTIONS

Step 1. First, remove the backing and current artwork and glass from the frame and set these aside.

Step 2. Give the frame a fresh coat of paint. You can do this with spray paint for an even finish, or use chalk paint for a more weathered, distressed look.

Step 3. Choose new artwork for the frame. Etsy is great for finding artwork that you can print out quickly and inexpensively. Depending on the size of your frame, most home printers will be able to print up to 8 × 10 artwork on cardstock beautifully. For larger prints, you will want to use a printing service like Mpix, where you can upload your photo online and choose the size you want to have it printed in. You can also visit your nearest office supply store for same-day or next-day printing.

Step 4. Once you've selected your artwork, if you're using the same matting from the original frame, determine if it needs to be refreshed as well. Chalk paint or mineral paint can completely transform the color of your mat so it coordinates better with the colors in your artwork. Most craft stores like Hobby Lobby and Michaels carry photo mats and can cut custom sizes on the spot.

Step 5. Once the paint on your frame and mat (if applied) is dry, begin assembling your thrifted frame back together. Be sure to clean both sides of the glass before putting it back in the frame so it looks brand-new again.

Step 6. Hang your repurposed treasure in the desired spot on your wall, or use it in a vignette or on your mantel to complete your seasonal look.

UNDERSTATED ELEGANCE

Adorning our hutch with understated elegance is one of the ways I transition our dining room over from summer to autumn. I don't go crazy with fall decor throughout our home but instead focus on a few key areas to highlight my seasonal favorites, including our dining room hutch. I incorporate serveware like my large oval antique silver platter that reminds me of Thanksgiving, since it resembles the platter we serve turkey on.

Since pumpkins are one of my favorite fall decor pieces, I start with those. I place them on cake stands and in bowls. To add height on the top shelf, I fill a large glass cloche with faux white pumpkins that contrast nicely with the wood tones of the hutch. You could use all white, like I do, or play around with different colors to suit your personal style.

Next, it's time to add some fall foliage. Since I gravitate toward the muted tones of fall, I use a variety of different leaves, stems, and dried pods in oranges and browns gathered together in a large white pitcher to add texture and a little bit of color. I place a pitcher full of branches off to one side, then tuck in a few of the same branches in the top shelf on the opposite side. Placing my foliage in a diagonal line across from each other adds balance to the overall display of my hutch versus if I were to place it all on the same side. Using a diagonal placement helps keep the eye moving while also bringing balance to the display.

Once I have the larger fall decor pieces and foliage in place, it's time to add a few little embellishments to finish things off. Since all my serving pieces on display are of the same material, I add in some cloth napkins to include a different texture. You can choose linens in seasonal prints or colors to further soften the look of your display. I also showcase my mini pumpkin salt and pepper shakers and some gold leaf napkin rings.

When it comes to choosing what to display, remember that those beautiful platters and crystal stemware don't have to be reserved only for Thanksgiving Day. Whether you are decorating a hutch or open shelves in your dining room or kitchen, you can display your treasured holiday serving pieces all season long.

A Harvest Bounty Planter

While pumpkins are my go-to choice for fall decor inside our home, I can't wait to add them to our front porch steps as well. I group them together in different sizes and place them on our front steps, around our seasonal planters. Inside our planters I like to display plants that come in different heights and offer different textures that contrast with the smooth, round pumpkins. Fountain grass that sways in the wind next to a compact ornamental kale represents signs of autumn's harvest. You might think that planting season is over come fall, but these fall planters are fuss-free and will take you from September right up to Thanksgiving.

Whether you are using three plants like I did, or more to fill a larger container, where you place your planter will determine how you assemble it. For planters placed up against a wall, you will want to arrange your plants in order by height, with the tallest plants in the back and the shortest in the front, so all the plants can be seen when you're viewing them from the front. If your planter is floating in an open space (not up against a wall), then you will want to place the tallest plants in the middle and the shortest plants around the outside edge so the same display is visible on all sides.

SUPPLIES

+ 1 planter
+ 1 bag of soil
+ 1 fountain grass
+ 1 mum or fall flower of your choice
+ 1 ornamental kale

DIRECTIONS

Step 1. Fill the planter with soil.

Step 2. Start by placing your tallest plant in the planter first. (I chose fountain grass.) This sets a backdrop for the shorter plants you will use.

Step 3. Once your tallest plant is in place, position your next tallest plant in the planter. (This was a mum in my display.)

Step 4. In the remaining open spot, place your shortest plant. (I used ornamental kale.)

CELEBRATE WITH INTENTION

And all at once, summer collapsed into fall.

OSCAR WILDE

I've learned over the years that I have to be intentional about focusing on ways to celebrate fall. With back-to-school comes fall sports and a busy schedule for our family, and our calendar has a way of filling up quickly. I am aware that if I'm not careful, our schedule will keep us so busy that, before we know it, the last leaf will have fallen and the holidays are upon us in a whirl of merriment and flurry. To ensure I don't arrive to the end of the season full of remorse that it ended before I got to really enjoy it, I look for ways to make fall meaningful all season long.

Being intentional about shifting into the fall season offers us the chance to incorporate new things into our daily lives. A new comfort-food recipe might quickly become a family favorite. Baking bread just seems right as the temperatures begin to cool. Be intentional about gathering with friends. Whether you host Thanksgiving or not, plan a potluck-style Friendsgiving, with each friend bringing their favorite Thanksgiving side dish. It keeps the gathering stress-free and takes the pressure off of having to prepare an entire meal by yourself. Plus, you get to learn a little more about your friends and their family traditions. Plan a fun fall family outing that can become a tradition, like going apple picking or tackling a corn maze together. I've learned as my kids have gotten older, it's not so much doing the same thing year after year but taking the time to do something special that helps us savor the season.

With the change that every new season brings, there will always be some sort of maintenance or upkeep that needs to be done around the house. But chores don't always have to feel like work. My kids are older now, but jumping into a pile of leaves is still one of their favorite things to do every autumn. Heck, even the dogs love it! Even though the kids are old enough to help us with this chore, no leaf-raking task is complete without the fun of playing in a few leaf piles.

Fall also brings with it the task of garden cleanup, and while we all enjoy the harvest our garden produces each year, not everyone enjoys getting the garden beds ready for winter. To encourage the kids to help out, we celebrate completing the task with a bonfire at the end of the day. In our house, that tends to be everyone's favorite outdoor activity.

When I take the time to slow down and find ways to celebrate the current season I'm in, I always find myself feeling full of contentment and joy, whether it's at work or at play. Making the season meaningful doesn't always have to be about adding more things to our schedule or spending more money. In the everyday moments when we intentionally look for ways to add meaning to our lives, we find ourselves enjoying and celebrating all the season has to offer.

What mood does the fall season spark in you?
How might that become part of your
theme of meaning this year?

fall inspiration list

GO FOR A DRIVE AND ADMIRE THE FALL FOLIAGE | VISIT A PUMPKIN PATCH AND CHOOSE YOUR FAVORITE PUMPKINS | GO APPLE PICKING | MAKE A PIE FROM SCRATCH | HOST A CHILI OR SOUP COOK-OFF | MAKE A FALL CRAFT | JUMP INTO A PILE OF LEAVES | WASH AND PUT AWAY OUTDOOR CUSHIONS | GO FOR A WALK IN THE WOODS AND DO A NATURE-THEMED SCAVENGER HUNT | CLEAN GARDEN TOOLS AND STORE THEM FOR THE WINTER | ATTEND A FAIR OR A FALL FESTIVAL | SWAP OUT FLORALS AND REPLACE THEM WITH FALL STEMS | BAKE HOMEMADE BREAD | HOST A POTLUCK FRIENDSGIVING | LIGHT A FALL-SCENTED CANDLE | SWAP OUT SUMMER BEDDING FOR COZY FLANNEL SHEETS | PRESERVE OR CAN VEGETABLES FROM YOUR GARDEN | ADD THROW BLANKETS AROUND YOUR HOUSE | DECORATE YOUR PORCH FOR FALL | MAKE A FALL-THEMED CRAFT | FILL THANKSGIVING BASKETS WITH CANNED GOODS AND DONATE THEM TO A LOCAL FOOD BANK | WEAR YOUR FAVORITE SWEATER OR INVEST IN A NEW ONE | TAKE A HAYRIDE | PLAY A BACKYARD GAME OF TOUCH FOOTBALL | WRITE DOWN A LIST OF THINGS YOU ARE THANKFUL FOR FROM THIS PAST YEAR

WINTER

If we begin to look at winter as a cozy season of respite, we can discover so many ways to delight in it.

WELCOME WINTER

Welcoming the season of winter into our homes can get lost in all the excitement of preparing for the holidays. Now, don't get me wrong, I love to decorate our home for Christmas, but what do we do once the holidays are over and all the holiday decorations are tucked away? There is so much more of the season to discover and savor. Yes, winter can get a bad rap, and it's no wonder. Typically, it's the coldest and darkest season of the year with shorter days, less sunlight, and maybe snow, depending on where you live. I love living in a region where we get to experience all four seasons, but living in New England also means our winter often continues well into March, making it feel like the longest season of the year.

It's easy to get excited about spring with the return of tiny buds on the trees and the first glimpses of green. Summer is anticipated for its long, warm days and unstructured schedule. And fall, perhaps the most anticipated season of all, offers its beautiful display of color along with the cool nights we gladly welcome after a hot or humid summer. I will be the first to admit that it took me a while before I could enjoy the beauty of winter.

First, I needed to understand the purpose of winter before I could truly embrace it in our home. During this time of the year, nature shows us how important it is to slow down. While the landscape around us hibernates, the soil has time to rest so it can replenish the nutrients needed to support growth in the coming season. You can do this in your home too. Think about setting up your spaces so they encourage you to slow down and rest. I consider which activities allow me to pause to take a breath and sit for a while, such as putting together a puzzle, relaxing by the fire, or settling into a favorite chair with a book and a hot beverage—all things that in warmer months get pushed aside for outdoor chores and activities. Taking a break with a soothing cup of tea, as simple as that sounds, is a ritual I enjoy only in the winter. If we begin to look at winter as a cozy season of respite, we can discover so many ways to delight in it.

I love to celebrate winter by focusing on the senses as I add seasonal decor to our home. When deciding what you want to add to your home during this season, think about what your senses are drawn to. Is there a certain scent that brings to mind cozy moments or a snow-covered trail? I have a balsam-and-cedar scented candle that I can't wait to light once winter arrives. Do certain textures inspire you to curl up and get cozy during the cold winter months? What foods and flavors do you crave? I like to stock my pantry with favorite teas and staple ingredients for comfort meals that warm us to the bone in winter. Even the songs that we listen to can help set the atmosphere in our home.

We miss out on so much beauty and peace if we limit our experience of winter to the month of December. When we learn to embrace the gifts the entire season has to offer, we will find ourselves appreciating the rest it brings and saying yes to its invitations to slow down and savor what is outside our windows and inside our comfy-as-a-favorite-sweater homes.

Let's embrace the entire season of winter together in simple, welcoming ways.

A HIDDEN VIBRANCY

Winter offers us an opportunity to rest—an invitation I want to reflect throughout our home all season long. Because the image of a white canvas of snow often represents winter on cards, paintings, and, in some regions, the actual landscape, winter is often perceived as being sterile and colorless. But I like to look to nature to reveal the hidden vibrancy of the season and decorate our home with this in mind. Evergreens and pine cones paired with knit textures are my go-to choices for the colder months. As I find peace in the stillness, I want to set up our home to offer comfort and warmth during the winter. And even if you live in a warmer climate, you can still highlight the coziness of the season.

Think about what represents winter to you. What scents do you love? Which color palettes are you drawn to? When looking around your spaces, consider how you can incorporate your favorite looks and textures that emulate winter. When transitioning our house from fall to winter, I like to swap out my autumn throw-pillow covers for ones with richer textures. Nothing says winter to me like chunky knits and fuzzy fabrics. I also replace the fall plaids and autumnal tones in my fabrics for darker greens that match the evergreen trees in my backyard. If we didn't swap out our sheets for flannels in the fall, we definitely swap them now and add extra blankets for winter. These small changes in textile choices are an easy way to ensure each room and nook is cozy for winter.

I take inventory of the rooms and spaces we gather in most and make sure they're stocked with everything we crave. In our house, everyone has their own throw blanket (or two), because we each prefer a different style and weight. I wash any blankets that have been sitting in baskets over the warmer months, so they're ready for those chilly nights. This way, when we curl up on the couch for family movie night, everyone gets to snuggle in comfortably together.

Blankets of varying textures also make wonderful holidays gifts. My kids love getting new fuzzy blankets (and so do I!), especially when their current ones have seen better days. Every couple of years they will find a brand-new blanket under the Christmas tree with their name on it. It's something they will enjoy for the rest of the season and beyond.

Since winter is the one season spent mostly indoors, I make sure that every room has what it needs to feel warm, welcoming, and snug in the best way. Typically, at the beginning of every new year, you will find the best sales on bedding. This is when I like to buy down blankets and new pillows to replace the ones that are worn out or no longer suit our home-decorating style.

Think about the fabrics and textures that say winter to you. How might the tones of the winter sky, berries, and trees be represented in the fabrics and linens throughout your home?

---

winter decor staples

EVERGREEN BRANCHES | PINE CONES | CANDLES | BOTTLEBRUSH TREES | CHUNKY KNIT BLANKETS AND PILLOW COVERS | TARNISHED ANTIQUE METAL URNS AND PLATTERS | MERCURY GLASS VOTIVES AND TREES | BIRCH TREE BRANCHES | FAUX FUR | FRESH OR FAUX JUNIPER BRANCHES

HOLIDAY MEETS NATURE

You can take on many different approaches with your winter vignette. You could create a display that is specifically meant for the holidays, with a themed piece of Christmas artwork or a special sign. Consider adding in nutcrackers and other traditional Christmas decorations to complete your look. Another approach would be to keep your vignette strictly winter-themed by keeping your focal point neutral—something you keep up all year long, such as a mirror or framed print that is not overly winter-specific. Bring in some pillar candlesticks and winter branches, and you'll be set for the entire season.

I styled my vignette with a mix of both Christmas and winter items, subtle holiday meets nature. Overall, the look is quite simple, with neutral artwork and a tiny bit of shimmer. But as we examine it more closely, you'll see how the two can blend together for a merry winter look.

I began by using double-sided tape to hang a large vintage-inspired tapestry centered above the hutch. The muted tones of the tapestry feel neutral and less like holiday decor. At first glance, it looks like a replica of an antique book page, but as you look closer, you can see the words from "The Christmas Song" printed on it, giving a subtle nod to the holiday. When I read the opening line—"Chestnuts roasting on an open fire"—my mind is instantly filled with warm memories of Christmas traditions.

To the left, I placed a cluster of various tabletop trees. While trees tend to have the same shape, I added variety by using trees with different finishes. You can choose trees that are the same or different. The key is to use trees of varying heights. If all your trees are the same height, place some of them on books or risers to give more dimension to your display. I've also put trees on tiny planter pots turned upside down to achieve a desired height.

I balance the vignette with a pedestal tray filled with walnuts and a sprig of greenery. This grouping is a nod to the lyrics in the tapestry.

Even though they aren't actually chestnuts, the shelled walnuts give a neutral alternative to colorful Christmas decorations.

I also added a grouping of antique brass candlesticks. Using candlesticks is one of my favorite ways to add height to a vignette, and the collection I purchased already came in different heights. Battery-operated taper candles are a good option for offering a worry-free soft glow to the room.

To bring in some elements from nature, I wove two strands of cedar garland around the decor. Without this addition, my display of mostly neutrals felt rather bare. The greenery really helped my vignette come to life while also adding a seasonal touch from the outdoors.

Tip: *If I get tired of my tabletop trees after Christmas, I can easily change things up by replacing them with a large vase or container filled with winter branches or stems. This preserves the height and balance of the vignette, while creating a shift from holiday-specific to a general winter feel.*

{DIY}

Reupholstered Footstool

There is nothing I love more than setting up cozy seating areas in the winter. Creating a space you can escape to with a mug of your favorite hot beverage and a blanket to curl up in is all I need to help me reset in the winter. There are a few things that make up this cozy seating area—a comfy chair, a fuzzy throw blanket, a little side table if there's room, and a footstool. This thrifted footstool needed a makeover, but I knew the bones were good and it would make the perfect addition to my cozy seating area. Here's what you need to get started restoring your own.

SUPPLIES

+ Upholstered footstool
+ Pliers
+ Furniture paint or stain, depending on your desired finished look for the footstool base
+ Batting
+ Approximately 2 yards of upholstery fabric (depending on the size of your footstool)
+ Foam (optional)
+ Staple gun

DIRECTIONS

Step 1. Begin by removing the original cushion from the base.

Step 2. Remove the original fabric and batting, but don't discard it yet! (I would also suggest replacing the original foam piece if there is one, as these can get quite stinky.)

Step 3. Using the pliers, remove any staples or nails that are used to hold the original fabric in place.

Step 4. Paint or stain the wood of the footstool base, depending on its condition and your desired look.

Step 5. Lay out your new fabric on a flat surface. Place the original fabric on top of the new fabric and use it as a template to cut the new fabric to the same size. Repeat this step with the batting (and new foam if this applies).

Step 6. Once the fabric and batting are cut to size, lay the new fabric right side down, then lay the batting on top, with the backer board of the footstool atop the batting. Begin by attaching the new batting to the backer board: Staple the batting to the center of the board, and then staple one side at a time, making sure to pull the batting taut as you go.

Step 7. Once the center of each side is secure, continue adding staples, pulling the batting taut as you go, until all sides are secured. Once the batting is attached, repeat Step 6 and Step 7 to attach the new fabric as well.

Step 8. To fold the corners, pull the fabric over to the left side of the corner, smoothing it out with your hands, and staple it on the printed side of the fabric to keep it in place. Then fold the fabric back over to the right side, smoothing out the corner as much as you can, and staple underneath to secure. Trim off any excess fabric.

Step 9. Once you've attached the new fabric to your footstool, attach the top to the base, and it's all ready for you to use!

{STEMS}

SPARSENESS & SIMPLICITY

While I will always prefer real greenery over faux in my home, I've realized that if I'm going to get through the winter months, I need some greenery that lasts and doesn't dry out. I've invested in quality faux options that I enjoy using all winter long. I still like to include some real cedar branches when I can, because nothing beats the scent of cedar.

Inevitably, my home feels a little empty when the Christmas tree comes down, but when I go to home decor stores in January and February, I'm bombarded with all things spring. And who isn't a bit ready for sprigs of bright green and colorful flowers after weeks of freezing temps? But personally, I've noticed that if I try to rush through winter and welcome spring too early, I resent winter even more. With cheery, sunny decor all throughout my home, I end up grumpy because nature hasn't gotten on board yet—as if I could force an early seasonal transition by the way I decorate my home.

In order for me to truly embrace winter and all it has to offer, I need to slow down and allow myself to soak in all its uniqueness. Once I started incorporating more winter greenery into my decor, whether in real or faux forms, I was able to enjoy the winter season longer instead of begrudgingly waiting for it to pass as soon as the stockings went back into storage. I have yet to meet a person who says winter is their favorite season, but I will say it is growing on me more and more, and I find myself looking forward to the slowdown that comes with winter. I am now able to find beauty in the sparseness and simplicity of the season.

Selecting stems that feel seasonally appropriate is key. Imagine how funny it would feel to fill a vase with fall branches in your home in the middle of winter. Seasonal stems add some life back into your spaces while still keeping the aesthetic clean and simple. There's nothing I love more than heading out into my backyard for a walk in the snow with clippers in my hand. Yes, I love to do this in any season, but I find it the most refreshing in winter as I search for a cluster of freshly cut branches to bring a breath of fresh air indoors.

If you don't have a backyard from which to clip some real offerings, head to your local nursery or garden center to find some fresh greens. And if you're in the market for some high-quality, realistic faux winter greens, Afloral and Terrain are some of my favorite places to shop online. I usually wait for the greens to go on sale, but the investment will last you year after year.

favorite stems and blooms

CEDAR | WHITE SNOWBERRY | SILVER BRUNIA | DUSTY MILLER | PINE | HELLEBORE | PAPERWHITES | WILLOW EUCALYPTUS | JUNIPER | BAY LEAF

Paperwhite Floral Arrangement

Paperwhites, typically known for blooming in the spring, are becoming just as popular as amaryllis during the holiday season. You can force paperwhite bulbs to bloom indoors any time of the year, and I love incorporating them into my winter decor because they can carry me all the way into spring. While you could also use real paperwhite bulbs to create this arrangement, using realistic faux bulbs makes this project fuss-free—plus you can use it year after year. This arrangement is perfect as the centerpiece that adds a pop of greenery to a table, buffet, or console table.

SUPPLIES

+ Dry floral foam bricks
+ Shallow bowl or urn
+ 3 to 4 faux paperwhite stems
+ 2 to 3 faux cedar stems
+ 2 to 3 faux juniper stems
+ Tiny ornaments (optional)

DIRECTIONS

Step 1. Place the dry floral foam in the base of your bowl. You can use a kitchen knife to cut the bricks so they fit securely in the bowl.

Step 2. Insert the paperwhite stems into the foam toward the center of the bowl. Create a square if using four stems and a triangle shape if using three. Leave a little bit of space in between each stem for the faux greenery. (You could leave a bit more if your stems also have the bulbs attached.) I like to place my stems standing straight up to keep consistent with how the flowers naturally grow.

Step 3. Next, place the winter greens around the outside of the stems, being sure to cover all the floral foam. Fill in any gaps where the floral foam is still visible—including in the center of the stems or bulbs—with a thicker foliage on top. I like to use cedar around the base and juniper on top to help cover any gaps.

Step 4. Sprinkle tiny ornaments around the base of the paperwhite bulbs for a little added sparkle.

{DIY}

Spruced-Up Store-Bought Wreath

I love to hang a fresh wreath on our door to greet guests for the holidays. One of my favorite winter hacks is to spruce up a store-bought wreath. You can usually find inexpensive ones at the grocery store or local Christmas tree stand. I grab a few different varieties of some of my favorite winter greens, such as eucalyptus and balsam, and before I know it, I've created a beautiful custom wreath. With minimal supplies, you can make your own too. Here's what you need.

SUPPLIES

+ 1 fresh store-bought wreath
+ 2 to 3 stems seeded eucalyptus
+ Floral wire
+ Wire cutters
+ 3 to 5 stems fresh balsam
+ 3 to 5 stems silver bell pods
+ Decorative ribbon

DIRECTIONS

Step 1. Begin by placing the store-bought wreath on a flat work surface.

Step 2. Cut the eucalyptus branches into individual stems. Working counter-clockwise, begin tucking them into the wreath, securing with floral wire if needed, and making sure they are evenly spaced.

Step 3. Add in sprigs of fresh balsam in between the eucalyptus stems to create a fuller looking wreath. Secure with floral wire if needed.

Step 4. Cut silver bell pods to 3 to 4 inches in length. Place them evenly around the wreath, filling in any remaining bare spots left from the balsam and eucalyptus.

Step 5. Attach a festive bow to the wreath with floral wire, then hang in desired place. I love to hang mine on my front door to greet guests, or layered on top of a mirror to add a festive touch.

CANDLELIGHT, COMFORT & COMPANY

Whether your home has holiday decorations displayed throughout or it's post-holiday and you're longing for some peace after the hustle and bustle, creating a simple tablescape can be just what you need to allow for a bit of breathing room, visually speaking. This tablescape provides ideal elegance for a formal sit-down gathering, simple beauty for a family meal, and the perfect festive decor for when the table isn't in use.

Gathering in the winter means I get to savor certain elements, scents, and flavors that help me better appreciate the season. The warm glow of candlelight on the table and the aroma and taste of comfort foods like hot soup and homemade bread fill me with joy for the season and gratitude for the company of those around our table.

CENTERPIECE

While fresh flowers are always my first choice, they are harder to come by during the winter months. Faux paperwhites offer the look of real flowers while requiring zero maintenance, so you can enjoy them all season long. They even help transition you into spring. You can see how I made this faux floral arrangement in this season of the book, so that you can re-create the same arrangement (see page 203).

HEIGHT & SILHOUETTE

On either side of the centerpiece, I place two wooden candlesticks in a diagonal line across from each other. I like to use different heights, placing the taller candlestick closest to the centerpiece and the shorter candlestick farther away. I also bring in cream-colored bottlebrush trees of varying heights and nestle them around the candlesticks, starting with the tallest ones closer to the center and working my way out so the shortest trees are on each end. Every winter I look forward to incorporating tabletop trees into my tablescapes during the winter season. I like to use bottlebrush trees, but for a simpler look, you could use shiny mercury glass trees to add elegance along with smaller potted bulbs or pillar candles for more ambiance. The key to a beautiful tablescape is using different heights, placing your decorating pieces in a zigzag line down the center of the table instead of in a straight line. This keeps the eye moving for more visual depth and delight.

PLACE SETTINGS

Since we are gathering indoors, I like to keep things a little more formal, which makes the winter months feel a bit more special. I bring out my inherited china set and heirloom silverware for an elegant touch to this simple table. Cotton napkins printed with winter greens reinforce the season we're in, while a tiny sprig of cedar and a mini pine cone on each place setting adds an extra seasonal touch.

STATEMENTS WITH STAYING POWER

Winter is my favorite time of year to decorate our fireplace mantel. Of course, one can't help thinking of Christmas stockings, chestnuts roasting, and all the other imagery inspired by a cheery fire. Our fireplace is the main focal point of our kitchen and dining room, so I love to make a statement with it during the holiday season. The key is to decorate it with pieces that can be left up well after the holidays are over. I like to change up my winter mantel from year to year, but the formula for how I go about decorating it stays basically the same: *focal point, seasonal greenery, height.*

As with every seasonal transition, I start by clearing off my mantel completely, so I have a clean slate to build on. Then I put up my focal point for that season. One of my favorite acquired pieces is a large "Rooms for Rent" sign made to look like an old mercantile sign. I love the style of it, and it's also the sign that inspired the name of my blog, so it holds a special place in my heart. You could use an antique ski lodge sign or a vintage Christmas tree farm sign. I've also used artwork that showcases a wintry scene. Go with whatever inspires you to create a focal point that reflects the season you're in and the mood you desire.

Next, I add bottlebrush trees in different heights and sizes, placing them on either end of my focal point. I start by placing my tallest trees closest to my sign and then working my way toward either end, finishing with my shortest trees. If you're struggling with how to place these, consider creating a layered look by placing a few smaller trees slightly in front of the taller trees in the back. This will add depth to your display and keep the arrangement from feeling flat.

With my bottlebrush trees in place, now I'm ready to add in some seasonal greenery. I always can't wait to hang my garland on our fireplace mantel. It's my favorite wintertime decor piece. While I love using real garlands throughout our home for Christmas, I invested in a realistic, high-quality faux garland for this feature piece. Since we have an actual wood-burning fireplace, I don't have to worry about this garland drying out and creating the mess a real one would. After securing the garland in place, I add in tiny embellishments such as faux juniper picks for a little contrast, followed by dried pods and pine cones foraged from our yard. Mixing in real or dried stems when using faux garland helps it look more realistic and provides a natural outdoorsy scent.

I like to finish off my winter mantel with two strands of wooden beads for a festive yet neutral touch. On Christmas Eve, we hang our knit stockings grouped together on one side. Once Christmas is over, the stockings and bead strands come down, but I still have a wintry mantel to enjoy until the signs of spring surface again.

{HUTCH}

COHESIVE & CURATED

If you find yourself overwhelmed with where to start decorating, pick an area that would be easiest or the most enjoyable to have done. Perhaps there is one surface in your home that you know exactly how you want to decorate. Start there and it will inspire you to tackle other areas.

My dining room hutch is that ideal starter space. I begin by adding some of my seasonal decor favorites—neutral bottlebrush trees that remind me of the snow-covered trees on our property and tiny white ceramic houses placed on top of cake stands or nestled next to bowls. This pairing creates the image of a tiny winter village on the shelves. Winter is the one season where I remove most of my staple serving pieces from the hutch. I do this to allow room to display some of my larger table-top trees (and, of course, those charming mini houses).

Whether you're decorating a hutch, open shelves, or a bookcase, focus on adding touches of greenery—real or faux. I drape a faux cedar garland over the top of the hutch and scatter cedar stems throughout the different shelves. The winter greenery adds a pop of color that provides a festive contrast to my white serving pieces and the rest of my winter decor. Clusters of white winterberries and pine cones add a natural touch and keep the overall look seasonally spot-on.

I do like to add in a little sparkle here and there. I fill bowls and urns with mercury glass ornaments and a few sprigs of greenery. It's an easy way to add a little shimmer without decorating our entire hutch or the open shelves specifically for Christmas. Grouping pieces in a bowl is a perfect opportunity to incorporate a particular color into your seasonal decor or to highlight some of your most treasured ornaments so they don't get lost among the other ornaments on the tree.

I use miniature bottlebrush trees in little groupings to finish things off. These can be found at craft stores and discount and department stores. They fit perfectly on top of stacked plates or on smaller shelves, making them a go-to when decorating the hutch or other surfaces. Using trees that are all in the same color palette adds a cohesive feel to the overall look of the display, making it feel less cluttered and more curated. A few scattered ornaments placed around my hutch add a little bit of sparkle for the holidays, yet can easily be put away once I'm ready for it to just feel like winter.

Displaying a collection of winter decor creates a cohesive look. Think of grouping together tiny trees, mini houses, Christmas dishes, or special serving pieces that you wish to highlight. Remember, it's all about balance. You don't need to remove all your everyday pieces. If you're decorating a bookcase, you still want it to look and function like a bookcase. The seasonal elements you add in should be an accent to the everyday pieces you already have on display.

{DIY}

Water-Free & Welcoming Planter

I love the ease of creating a container arrangement in winter without having to worry about watering it. Cold temperatures outside keep these clipped evergreen boughs fresh for months. Just be careful not to leave your containers in direct sunlight for too long or they will start to look crispy. This winter-themed planter next to our front door is just the welcome I want to convey as we move through the winter season.

SUPPLIES

+ 1 planter
+ 1 bag of soil
+ Cedar boughs
+ Juniper branches
+ Birch branches 1 to 1½ inches in diameter, 17 to 18 inches long
+ Pine cones or other decorating elements such as seed pods or berries

DIRECTIONS

Step 1. Fill the planter with soil.

Step 2. Begin by creating a base layer with evergreens. I place cedar boughs along the outside circle of the planter, gently pressing the stems into the soil.

Step 3. Place your birch branches into the container in a triangle shape. Secure them in the soil so they don't tip over.

Step 4. Add in more cedar boughs around the birch branches, covering most of the exposed soil in the middle of your planter and putting the taller branches in the back and the shorter branches toward the front.

Step 5. Next, evenly place juniper branches throughout the planter. I like to start by placing one stem in front of each birch branch and then filling in with a few more in the middle.

Step 6. Add in your favorite decorative elements. I added pine cones and silver bell seed pods to add some visual contrast and depth to my arrangement.

ABOUT THE AUTHOR

Bre Doucette is the author of *The Gift of Gathering* and *The Gift of Home* and the creative founder and writer behind the blog *Rooms for Rent,* with its signature simple approach to design. She decorates with her heart and believes that whether you rent or own your home, whether you're an empty nester or a first-apartment dweller, you can love the space you live in.

Bre has been featured in *Better Homes & Gardens, Country Living, House Beautiful, Good Housekeeping, Yankee, Country Home,* and *Country Woman.* Her passion is to inspire women not only in their homes but also in their creative dreams. "Whether I'm decorating our home for my family or inspiring other women to enjoy their spaces, I love serving others through the gifts God has given me. Wherever you are in your journey, I hope you feel inspired and encouraged to embrace the gifts God has given you so you can bless those in your circles too!"

For more inspiration, connect with and follow Bre at
www.roomsforrentblog.com
Instagram @roomsforrent

winter inspiration list

GO THROUGH HATS, GLOVES, AND SCARVES AND SEE WHAT'S MISSING. PURCHASE ANY NEW ITEMS YOU NEED AT POST-HOLIDAY SALES | ORGANIZE YOUR WINTER GEAR SO IT'S READY FOR USE WHEN INSPIRATION STRIKES | PUT AWAY HOLIDAY-FOCUSED ITEMS WHILE KEEPING WINTER-THEMED DECOR OUT | CLEAN OFF ALL SURFACES SO YOU START WITH A CLEAN SLATE | KEEP BASKETS STOCKED WITH CHUNKY THROW BLANKETS | ORGANIZE AND CLEAN OUT DRAWERS | DESIGNATE AN AREA OR NOOK FOR BOARD GAMES AND PUZZLES | MAKE A WINTER-THEMED CRAFT | USE TABLE LAMPS AND OTHER PLEASANT LIGHT SOURCES SUCH AS CANDLES | TACKLE A PROJECT OR TWO AROUND THE HOUSE | DREAM OF WARMER DAYS BY PLANNING YOUR SPRING GARDEN | PUT TOGETHER A PUZZLE | SIP A CUP OF TEA AND ENJOY THE VIEW OUTSIDE YOUR WINDOW | MAKE YOUR FAVORITE WINTER MEAL | TAKE A BUBBLE BATH BY CANDLELIGHT | JOURNAL YOUR GOALS AND PLANS FOR THE NEW YEAR | ENJOY AN OUTDOOR ACTIVITY | TRY A NEW HOBBY OR CRAFT | HAVE A MOVIE MARATHON | PLAY BOARD GAMES WITH FAMILY OR FRIENDS | INVEST IN COZY PJ'S FOR THE WHOLE FAMILY | MAKE HOMEMADE HOT COCOA | READ A NEW BOOK | LIGHT A WINTER-SCENTED CANDLE | HOST A GIRLS' NIGHT IN AND SWAP YOUR FAVORITE COOKIE RECIPES

While I love the fresh start that comes with the new year, I try to let my house be somewhat at rest. I do this by keeping minimal decor to provide a visual clean slate. Then, I create a cozy environment that serves the shorter days by incorporating soft lighting such as candles and table lamps. I set the tone in the house so the family can enjoy—and even appreciate—the rest of the winter season and embrace the early sunsets and chilly yet cozy evenings. As I take the time to style these intentional spaces, I find myself looking forward to this time of the year more and more.

Post-holiday, which decor elements do you want to keep out to reflect winter's beauty and mood? What activities and hobbies might you and your family enjoy this time of year? What might be missing in some of your spaces that would help you enjoy winter more?

COZY CORNERS & COMMON AREAS

He who marvels at the beauty of the world in summer will find equal cause for wonder and admiration in winter.

JOHN BURROUGHS

Winter can seem very long and the family can start to feel a bit stir-crazy, so I make sure our home is set up to provide an enjoyable, comfortable, and entertaining season of nesting. During most of the year, my family spends their time outdoors as much as possible, so when the colder months hit, I create areas in our common living spaces where we can gather around board games or a puzzle. Oftentimes the choice is to sit around our dining room table, but it is also fun to find an empty nook that can accommodate a small card table.

I realized one reason I wasn't fully embracing winter is that I wasn't partaking in any hobbies. By creating a "cozy corner," I—and the rest of my family—was drawn to a winter activity or two. Leaving out puzzles or sketchpads with colored pencils and markers or a basket of craft supplies encourages creativity, self-entertainment, and conversation.

Creating intentional spaces helps foster joy and connection in the home. Keeping those spaces (somewhat) clean will bring calm and peace. Unlike fall nesting, which I do at the start of the season, my winter nesting takes place in the middle of the season.

Once the magical holiday dust has settled, I like to do a little tidying up. I refresh and rearrange the winter decor I choose to leave out, vacuum up the dust bunnies, wipe down surfaces, and take some time to reorganize our home for the second half of winter.